Praise for **The Anomaly Mind-Set**

The Anomaly Mind-Set is a game changer. This book is full
of wisdom from the beginning to the end. Sandy Krakowski
is uniquely qualified to write about the truths concerning
business. This book will help you break out of that feeling
stuck place and change your small mind-set, and you
will begin to dream big again. It will give you direction.
The Anomaly Mind-Set is a book full of hope and
encouragement. Your life will forever be changed."

— **Kimberly Jones-Pothier**, Real Talk Kim, best-selling
author and radical preacher

"You have to read this book. In the first few paragraphs,
I was hooked. You feel seen, heard, and motivated all at
the same time. Truly, if you want your heart to open and
to have access to the power to create anything you want,
read this book. Underline it, study it but most of all allow
Sandi's words to lift you to an entirely new level. These
words are anointed . . . you can feel it."

— **Shanda Sumpter**, Queen Visionary of HeartCore Business

"I wish I had this book 25 years ago—it would have
saved me countless journeys of fear. Sandi's vulnerability
and self-awareness will help give you an attitude
that anything is possible."

— **Shawn Bolz**, host of Exploring the Prophetic podcast and
author of *Translating God*, *God Secrets*, and *Keys to Heaven's Economy*

"*The Anomaly Mind-Set* delivers a powerful message for anyone who has ever felt like an outsider: you *are* different and it's your greatest asset."

— **Mary O'Donohue**, media coach for authors, best-selling author, and former post producer at *The Oprah Winfrey Show*

"*The Anomaly Mind-Set* gives an inside look at how Sandi built multiple businesses by deviating from the usual. More than a business or self-help manual, this book is infused with hard-hitting honesty and candor about faith and the role it plays in Sandi's work. As a self-described 'spiritual unicorn,' she invites heaven into every strategy. If you find yourself stuck in the mundane and don't seem to be gaining traction, these principles are sure to launch you forward. *The Anomaly Mind-Set* will fundamentally change the way you live and lead."

— **Caleb Johnson**, writer, storyteller, and illusionist

THE
ANOMALY
MIND-SET

SANDI KRAKOWSKI

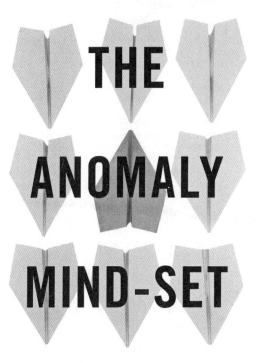

THE ANOMALY MIND-SET

HOW I TRANSFORMED MY BUSINESS
AND MY LIFE BY STANDING OUT
INSTEAD OF FITTING IN

HAY HOUSE, INC
Carlsbad, California • New York City
London • Sydney • New Delhi

Published in the United States by: Hay House, Inc.: www.hayhouse.com®
Published in Australia by: Hay House Australia Pty. Ltd.: www.hayhouse.com.au
Published in the United Kingdom by: Hay House UK, Ltd.: www.hayhouse.co.uk
Published in India by: Hay House Publishers India: www.hayhouse.co.in

Cover design: Jason Gabbert • *Interior design:* Nick C. Welch

Cataloging-in-Publication Data is on file at the Library of Congress

Hardcover ISBN: 978-1-4019-5645-5
E-book ISBN: 978-1-4019-5646-2
Audiobook ISBN: 978-1-4019-5674-5

10 9 8 7 6 5 4 3 2 1
1st edition, May 2019

Printed in the United States of America

*To the God of the Universe who made me
a unicorn who was never meant to fit in.
You are my life. Thank you for becoming
the Papa I longed for all along.*

ALSO BY SANDI KRAKOWSKI

#BeMore: 77 Secrets to Your Powerful Life

CONTENTS

FOREWORD

When I met Sandi, we were either going to go forward and break through, or we were going to break down and have to do something else other than our dream. She has a unique ability to let her courage, faith, and process rub off on everyone around her. We did break through, and her advice on our new beginning in 2015 was key. I went on to have my first international bestselling book, and within a short time we published 27 projects, and our books are bestsellers in our genre on Amazon, Barnes & Noble, and Christian booksellers everywhere. Sandi helped to break open our view of marketing and what was available but not just as a market expert. She spoke into the identity of our process and connected us to the language to harness our audience with a unique, love-based approach, not just an earning approach.

I just got done with her book and I love it because it captures something. It captures her internal process that she has paid a huge price to refine and develop after so many life hardships. She has become unrecognizable from her past, but it's because she did incredible work to believe and push herself with her faith, incredible discipline, and her self-care, which in a trifecta are so absent from most successful people.

I have always felt like somewhat of an anomaly as well, but I love how she took the stigma out of the word and it will take insecurity out of you! I felt like an anomaly, both in my natural pursuit of doing things that I am not always trained or skilled at, but also in my leadership and public speaking. I wish I had this book when I started 25-plus years ago—it would have saved me countless journeys of fear. Her book is such a great branding device of courage.

Sandi's vulnerability and self-awareness that has come out of her process is going to help give you an attitude that anything is possible, and that you don't have to be the sharpest knife in the drawer—you just have to have the identity to use who you are well.

There is a theme in the Bible that God uses the ones who are not qualified by natural means because He can show His love to the world that if He adds Himself we will get a different result and it will confound the wisdom of man. Sandi defines being this kind of person, and she calls it a unicorn. I own that I am one of those, and her book made me excited to see what could happen if a bunch of people would just believe in the success that God intends for us.

You are limitless, and you are, as she describes, a unicorn. Let this book help you commit to the process of becoming a success at being a true anomaly.

Shawn Bolz, host of Exploring the
Prophetic podcast and author of
Translating God, God Secrets, and
Keys to Heaven's Economy

INTRODUCTION

When I first set out to write this book, my mind was in a flurry (*which is not too uncommon for me*), but inside that flurry were so many broken pieces, fragments, and supernatural events, that finding where to start was like hunting for a dime in a haystack. Or a penny in a sand pile. It was hard. No, actually, it was excruciating.

Every step of my career has demanded that I break through stereotypes and mind-sets that have been upheld as "normal" for many, many years. I battled religious stereotypes that said to make millions of dollars with your only goal being to give it away, as well as societal stereotypes that said a woman can't have a successful business and have a great life as a mother at the same time. Being judged, lied about, spoken against—and in some cases, even attacked—for my perspective was preferable to staying put, because the pain of being stuck was far greater than any risk I'd ever encounter. It's been worth it, and it *will* be worth it for you too. Refusing to quit and being willing to take risks that may seem terrifying at times are the very things that could propel you into a future you were made for yet never before imagined.

You see, when I tell my story of making my first million by the time I was 30, my biggest challenge is retracing my footsteps and trying to figure out how I did it. That happens often with our genius. We'll do what we're best at, whether it's business, sports, modeling, writing, or balancing books, and many times when we're not even thinking about trying to be our best. I always tell my students to build a business (and a life!) around the things that you love, what comes naturally and instinctively. Don't build a career around something you have to strive and strain in. Looking back, I think my turning point was when I stopped caring what people thought, and made a decision to really be who I was created to be. This meant I'd raise my children how I wanted to, grooming and training them for success and not failure. I would also live my schedule how I wanted, which was very unconventional. Having a challenge in your work is great, but striving to be something you're not is toxic.

It didn't even dawn on me that the way I communicated with the spiritual world and Papa God was out of the ordinary. I wasn't really trying to be like anyone else; my pursuit was finding out how I could flourish on my own. That meant inviting Papa, the angels, and the entire spiritual realm into my work. This is what I did when I struggled as a mom and wife, so it was just natural for me to do this at work. I didn't realize this wasn't politically correct, or that it was out of the ordinary or even threatening until people started planting that kind of nonsense into my head. My truest self is as a businesswoman who is creative, spiritual, prophetic, insightful, and playful all wrapped up in one. The more I showed the world and business community my truest, authentic self, doors opened for me in ways I never dreamed were possible. But it wasn't easy. I was met with rejection, fear, judgment, worry, and more. Could it be that because deep in my heart, which still had the residue of trauma from my past, I expected these things to show up?

I want to ask you the same question. Do you expect the worst or plan for the best? Has your childhood pain plagued you as you've tried to move forward in your business? As you'll see on this journey with me of being an anomaly, the soul of your company, the core of everything, is going to be tied to you, the business owner. You are its greatest asset, whether you feel like it or not. Making the investment to work on yourself more than you do anything else will open up things inside you that might have been buried for a long time. It might surprise you that those things you might have been trying to change to be "more relatable" or "like everyone else" are actually expressions of the brilliant, anomaly genius we were born to fulfill! Work on yourself, as you work in your business, to release whatever that special quality is.

My own fears almost paralyzed me. Communicating things to others in the way that I was seeing them became a place of conflict, as people would look at me like a deer in headlights, not understanding anything I said. This made me feel insecure and devalued. While I had been instinctive and naturally wired to bring things together in business, my ability to communicate, to work with others, and to build a strong team wouldn't come until many years later. This is why I felt so strongly about writing this book. There are millions of you out there who feel the same. It wasn't until I met several other anomalies in the business world, and a few patient and powerful people who showed me that my uniqueness was exceptional, that I began to see that everyone has this same uniqueness. The quirks and things we think of as odd and set us apart could be the stepping-stones to a career. I had to heal enough to find that powerful communicator inside of me. My transformation would release that incredible team builder within—that and being a mother. HA! I'm laughing out loud. Raising three sons and homeschooling all three of them while I was building my companies taught me a lot about team building. Building my business revealed to me that I was never created to fit in a box, nor was I to be defined by typical standards. Rather, I was made to deviate from the typical system of business, creating my own unique way of doing things. This is being an anomaly: to go outside the boundaries, deviate from the norm, and to find what we've longed for all along.

It was a battle I fought while trying to find myself. Ironically, it ended up being the thing that showed me my greatest potential and that fitting in was never the design of my life.

Learning to accept your "quirks" and differences, seeing the things you have been trying to change as assets and not hinderances, and then opening yourself up to the anomaly genius that lies within will transform your life. You'll find a life filled with ease, one that was "waiting for you all along" as you fought your war. And you'll see that being an anomaly is an honor and a privilege, rather than a hinderance or a curse. I was created to share my gifts with the world and that includes all the unique, different, deviant, and wild ways of me, and I believe for you as well.

I am you. You are me. It is for us that I wrote this book! We are in this together!

I am you. You are me. It is for us that I wrote this book! We are in this together!

As I sit here, in the early hours of the morning, my heart is full of gratitude. I love you, my friend. We're so alike. I'm writing this book for all of us. You are why I am able to do what I do. Though we may have never met, I know you. You never give up! You keep pushing forward. You keep believing, even through seasons of dark unbelief and fear. You keep holding on even when everyone else would have quit a long, long time ago. It's because of you that I found the courage to write, so that I could share some of the incredible events, treasures, and supernatural experiences that have shaped my life and my business. When we see how we're all designed to not fit in but to live in beautiful harmony together, you'll see that other anomalies inspire, motivate, and even give you courage as they press forward on their path.

When I was growing up, depression, anxiety, and fear were my constant friends. While other little girls were having tea parties together, my three constant companions and I were doing our best to navigate through life in an abusive environment of religion, belittlement, perfectionism, abandonment, and fear. I'm still trying to figure out how I got here or why Papa God would even use a woman like me—but nevertheless, He did. And . . . here I am. Whether you believe in God or not, whether you care about the spiritual world or not, I want my anomaly journey to inspire you. Maybe you've also lived through abuse, neglect, or abandonment. Or you've experienced loss to a point that you find it extremely difficult to see the best in anything. You could be the person who suffered no abuse, was never taught by lack, and lived in what many have called a "perfect life"; but you have no clue who you are or what you really want to do with your life. Welcome aboard! All of you are welcome and more.

This book is going to open your heart and your mind to how all those things that make you feel like you don't fit in and are different are actually what make you powerful and destined for something great. It's the great battle and dichotomy, separating what we've always known or believed from all that we were designed to do. For me, bringing the supernatural into every area of my life gave me the courage to let all my quirks and twists become more public. I stopped trying to be like everyone else. As I walk in the spiritual throughout my day, heaven is very present and willing to permeate every aspect of my life and business. It's helped me discover how to go from being one of the most unlikely suspects for huge success in life to having my dreams come true. Dreams. You might as well just go there. All your dreams will come true, because that is what I've experienced. I don't believe that Papa God is playing favorites with anyone. You can have it too. But it will look like your life, *not mine.* We are alike, you and I, but our stories intersect in unique ways. So you being you and me being me *is crucial* for this to really play out as it's supposed to.

My life doesn't add up. I wasn't mentored for success or groomed to be powerful, and I wasn't okay with the idea of standing alone for more than half of my life. How does a girl who felt like an outcast most of the time—who was gang-raped in her 20s, was abused as a little girl, felt like a loner in school, and has been working hard to chameleonize herself for many years—become an influencer that people trust? How does someone who felt unsafe around most people become an encouraging voice for millions? Maybe you didn't experience trauma and pain like I did, but you might have always felt different, like you didn't belong. Maybe you've tested as being on the autism spectrum and have felt even more like an outcast, a deviant, one who departs from the norm . . . and you have no intention of ever going back. I tested as being in the range for high-functioning autism, or Asperger's, so I really get what it's like to be "exceptional" in some areas of life and nearly incompetent in others. My genius causes me to see trends and patterns in everything, but it also used to keep me tongue-tied, unable to convey to others all the pictures that danced in my head. As I began to grow my business, discover myself, and learn to walk in my truth, it was then that I realized my brain was exceptional, not broken; it was remarkable and beautiful, not weird or unsafe. All that test did was confirm to me that I was an anomaly and that this book needed to be written. Actually, I was thrilled to take the test because it made sense of so many things that didn't make sense before, such as my need for people one minute and my need to be alone with no interruptions the next!

If you feel like an anomaly, and you have had a life of pain and suffering and struggle, my heart goes out to you. In this book, my goal is to encourage you so you know that you too can have a life that is limitless. In your professional, your personal, and your spiritual life, I'm going to show you how the challenge of "not fitting in" is not only the key to unlocking your enormous potential, it's your greatest asset. When we are just surviving, we can't dream. But when we get beyond survival, into living our life as our truest anomaly self, it is my belief that nothing is impossible!

CHAPTER 1

THE UNLIKELY MILLIONAIRE

I knew I wanted to be a millionaire when I was seven years old. I remember receiving a chalkboard for my birthday that year. It became my favorite gift of all because to me it was more than a chalkboard: it was the launchpad for my dreams. Standing in front of it, I would imagine myself as a teacher, a leader, and even the owner of my own company. That simple gift allowed my little-girl mind to escape to worlds unknown. In the evenings, I'd pretend I was grading papers. My "students" were stuffed animals and dolls. The homework papers were, of course, pages I colored and wrote on and would then critique and "grade." The memory of how anything felt possible in that moment comes back quickly.

As I got older, my imagination grew, and so did my dreams. But where I saw endless possibilities, it always seemed the people around me saw limits. I'd dream of making my life bigger, getting a new house, trying new things I'd never done before. And I'd get comments like:

Don't get your hopes up so high—that's for kids.

Be more realistic!

You're just a dreamer.

Followed by such advice as:

Limits were set in place so that we don't get ourselves into trouble.

If you dream big, you'll find trouble.

Just stay content with what you have and be grateful.

This was the common way of living I saw around me. And I was supposed to do the same.

Except I couldn't.

Because deep down, *I knew I wasn't made to be limited.*

And so, the battle began between who I knew Papa had created me to be—a unique, creative, powerful, outside-the-box groundbreaker—and who I was expected to be: a nondisruptive, accepting, quiet conformist. Have you felt this war as well?

I was still a child, and soon the voices of the crowd began to drown out the dreams in my little heart, and fear became the replacement. The message was, "You don't fit in. You don't belong. You're different, broken because you think differently. You're always dreaming. You're not like us and aren't allowed to play with us." By the time I was 12, I had already encountered someone who made me terrified to be different. I was in the sixth grade and somewhat of an introvert. I hadn't yet found my ability to speak up, be myself, and shine. The memory comes back to me so clearly that as I write it out here, my heart begins to race a little bit. I can see Colleen's face of hatred. She is standing at the end of the hallway near my next class, talking to three other girls. She is a shorter girl, with a chest the size of a grown woman, but she's also in the sixth grade. People referred to her as a "leader," and I was told by one girl to never get in a hallway alone with her or she'd hurt me. How she'd hurt me wasn't quite clear, but as I approached my classroom that morning, she started walking toward me. These words came out of her mouth: "You think you're so good and so perfect. Look at you, carrying a purse in the sixth grade like li'l Miss High and Mighty. Well, if you cross my path one more time, bitch, I'll kill you. You don't belong here, and you are bothering me and everyone else in this school with that smile of yours!"

I was being bullied by a 12-year-old student with a 38D cup size. Here was a girl who was created beautifully unique and could have been a powerful voice for other girls, but in her effort to fight the fear of NOT fitting in, she succumbed to being a bully. She scared the crap out of me. To this day I still don't know why she was so threatened by me. I was pretty quiet in school, but always took hours every morning to look my best, be attractive, and to get to class on time. But after this encounter, I remember not wanting to go to school at all. I loved school and I really loved learning, but now I didn't want to stand out. I wanted—I needed—to fit in. The pain became so great that by the end of that school year I was hospitalized for the first time with a bleeding ulcer. Stomach problems followed, later diagnosed as ulcerative colitis, and then multiple other autoimmune conditions fought me for most of my life. It is my belief that the early trauma I experienced as a little girl in a place that I loved (school) set me up for "digesting" my feelings and "stuffing" my best self and thoughts. It made me sick. Literally sick.

The fear I encountered at school began to destroy my love for learning. The encounter in middle school created a muscle memory of sheer terror, absolute fear for my life that went through my whole body and made me want to run to safety. I was designed to love learning, be curious, poke around, investigate, and break things, even in my learning process. But the fear and insecurity of not fitting in made school a nightmare for me. The more I wanted to learn, the more I was questioned for my desire to learn more than the average student. The more I sought to go outside the lines as I am designed to do, the more my fear of people not getting me, my not fitting in, and my pain seemed to grow.

FREEDOM

You see, my story doesn't start with me on the fast track to success from childhood, raised in a home filled with encouragement, support, and love. I was never taught that I had greatness inside me, or that my creative, innovative, dreaming mind would make me a great fit for entrepreneurship, or that all of heaven was cheering me on. The idea that I could actually become everything I was designed to be and could impact lives by doing so never even entered my mind or my heart. My childhood was spent in fear and pain. Being sexually molested as a little girl and later feeling like I didn't fit in anywhere created confusion in my little mind. Struggle, sabotage, and pain were a part of what I pretty much believed was normal living. One of my biggest goals, starting at the age of 14, was to get out, leave the nightmare, and make some money so I could just live on my own.

I didn't realize until many, many years later that this desire to "just be on my own" and "fly on my own" was actually a part of my wiring as a pioneer. It's what makes me want to go solo when everyone is pulling me down. I would later discover in high school and my early 20s that when I felt trapped, or couldn't figure something out, I could reinvent how things are done and do it my way! For example, I got into bodybuilding in my senior year of high school, and competed for a few years. But the traditional way that people trained, worked out, and eventually go into competing didn't make sense to me. So I created my own fast track to success by inventing my own kind of workouts from examples gleaned from the piles of books I would study late into the night. That path of learning, to become saturated in a topic and then reinvent what I studied, became my MO for finding success later on. Even now, it's what gives me courage to invent new paths when the old ones are boring or simply don't make sense to me.

Each of us anomalies has a deep call for freedom woven into our DNA. We may feel like the very thing we're wired for has caused us the most grief or judgment in our lives. But there's always this fire, this thing inside of us that won't quit no matter how many times we give up. It's like a world inside of us is crying out to come to life, and many times, it's the thing that causes us the most opposition and trouble. I have met this deep cry to be free in countless individuals who have come to our events or who are in my Inner Circle mastermind. They know there's more, and they're fighting internally to find their way.

It's why we buck things that hold us back. Sadly, it's also why, if we're not careful, we can create self-imposed prisons that we fit ourselves into just so we can feel like we belong. A distorted, unhealthy view of this call for freedom can lead many of us to succumb to an erroneous belief that living in a predictable box is freedom, when every attempt we've made to fly ends up in tragedy. That business we might try to start is met with financial challenges, lack of skill, or maybe more is required of our time than some "you can be successful too" ad promised us. Before we know it, we're okay with our 9 to 5, because "at least" it brings us a paycheck; it's something we can still control, and with a smile on our face, just do day in and day out. Soon we're striving to control our lives just enough that nothing unpredictable, outside the box, or uncomfortable happens, and we begin to think this is freedom. *No, this is the high end of status quo,* when we have a few things in life we dreamed about but don't make too many waves, and we're rarely experiencing any kind of opposition. How did we ever get to a place where opposition is supposed to be feared and being passive is to be revered? That's a question I ask my students in my mastermind a lot, because many tend to come to me in a sleepy stupor, feeling like their greatness has been drained out and replaced with "just survive."

But it is in the opposition, my friend, *in the deep end of finding who we are* and walking out our desires that we meet a world of ideas, innovations, dreams, and even unspoken intentions that could change us forever. This is what I refer to as "resistance." It's a term meaning opposition. It's not always someone or something, like demons, enemies, and the like. It can just be the chatter inside of our own heads that we're so accustomed to that we back down anytime it raises its voice.

This is why we need each other. I need your story as much as you need mine for us to become all that we were created to be. This is also why not fitting in can be the key—the dividing line of those who will and those who won't see success beyond anything we've ever imagined. What do I mean by this? The world seems to have its system: a plan, method, or way we're supposed to follow to find happiness, financial security, peace of mind, harmony, and contentment. It's almost as if we are programmed to hate that with which we are wired. It's like there's this silent undercurrent of opposition that says, "Don't rise up, don't be big, don't fight forward—just lie down." Just one check of the statistics for overdoses, alcoholism, and the amount of people on antidepressant drugs and it's obvious that this so-called system is not helping us at all. It's a method of control, one where things don't happen that are unpredictable or, God forbid, *messy*! This is why I began to realize that the very thing many of us fight, and try to pacify, silence, and eliminate, could be the very thing that leads us to either our truest gifts and power, or *it is in and of itself one of our greatest strengths.*

In adulthood I would discover, by the grace of God and a lot of healing on my part, that the very things that got me into trouble, made me not fit in, and caused me to want to run away— talking all the time, thinking of brilliant things in a random second, and the ability to be very articulate and analytical but also crazy creative and inspirational—are *the very things that people now say shine through as my most genuine self*! It is the *exact* thing that Papa had wired me for. It's how I'm created and what I was uniquely designed to be. It is the "anomaly factor" of my success in life, and has become the linchpin of many of the things I'm known for today.

THE ANOMALY'S PATH

Unfortunately for many of us who are wired differently, we live in a system created by people who want to be in control. If you buck the system or are created in such a way that you can't align with such systems, you will be marked as trouble at an early age. This same system tried to medicate, inoculate against, and shut off my own creativity when I was 20.

I felt like I could no longer live with the voices in my head that said to dream, explore, and create, while the voices in my life outside my head said to settle, be practical, and slow down. My first feelings of a nervous breakdown were panic followed by an intense desire to just sleep. Sleep for years. Being a single mommy seemed to set me up for inviting a lot of unwanted advice and opinions. Some people thought that I should go off and get a good job. Others thought I should put my son in daycare, rather than taking him with me as I ran my cleaning business. The apartment I chose, was it good enough? Safe enough? Was I providing my child with the things he needed to grow up to live like the other kids? That, I would later discover, was the question all along. The very same "Stop bucking the system and living so outside our boxes" mentality that I was confronted with as a child again raised its ugly face when parenting my son became my sole focus.

But raising him like everyone else raised their kids was never my goal. Making sure he was safe was always a priority, but sadly, the desire to give him everything he needed to be his own creative self was met with constant criticism. I gave in, and *almost gave up* when I was hospitalized for a full-blown shutdown (nervous breakdown).

Isn't it ironic that the same system that should have protected me and my son neglected to ask about my own trauma? They worked really hard to keep me in a box. I remember one extremely unintelligent doctor asking me if I was "manic" because I had a red shirt on one day. Waking up in the hospital feeling vibrant, alive, and full of life again, I chose a shirt that showed how I felt—bright, flaming red! But his professional and medical opinion was that this actually showed I was unstable, extreme, and manic. Out of my mouth flew words I'll never forget as long as I live. "Oh, really? So that means that the black shirt you choose to wear today means you're obsessed with death? Yeah. I thought so." And I walked away. Later that day I checked myself out voluntarily, and had to sign a million waivers making sure I'd protect myself and be okay. It was almost like signing a contract that validated I was not going to listen to the system and was going to fly on my own. I wasn't manic; I was a fire-breathing unicorn who was trying to find herself but gave into pressure and tried to fit into boxes she was never made for.

What is your box that you run to and hide in? Are you pacifying, silencing, and trying to fight all the things you were created for? Listen, I understand. Manic depression is a serious condition. But checking myself out was a wise decision, not irresponsible. How did I know? Because all my labs, tests, and so on always came back negative for anything serious. ALWAYS. I was a perplexing anomaly to even the doctors who tried to medicate the genius out of me.

Just two years later, after working with several amazing doctors who would grow to understand who I am and how I am wired, and some spiritual leaders as well, I would stand before a board of psychiatrists explaining to them that I wanted to start my own business, was well able to provide for myself, and no longer needed government funding for the "depression" that had incapacitated me. There was a system set up for people who couldn't work, and some well-meaning but very stupid people had talked me into just accepting that I wasn't normal and that my "condition" was why I was so extreme. Now listen to me here, I understand real depression. I understand chemical depression as well. I've had both, and know that when hormones and brain chemistry get all out of balance, so will we. But this was not the case. I was a young woman striving to be different and reaching for my own identity and raising my young son, and yet the trauma I had experienced as a young girl kept surfacing to disable me. Add to that people who told me to not be so hard on myself and just realize that this might be how my life plays out, and I quit. But all I needed was just a week locked up in such a facility with people who can't take care of themselves, think on their own, or protect themselves, and I soon realized this was NOT the case with me. Medication after medication and even electroconvulsive therapy didn't change my desire to fly and be my own person! I thank Papa daily that these things didn't permanently damage my amazing, beautiful mind. Little did anyone know at the time that I'd make millions of dollars just 10 short years later and have a life that even I didn't plan for.

We anomalies were not made to fit into preconceived boxes, or to govern our lives according to what society deems as normal and typical. No, we're the box breakers, the boundary pushers, the rule breakers who are made to challenge the status quo and get people to rethink "normal." We don't want to behave, and we don't need to answer every critical voice that rises up. What we *do* need to do is become the best person we can become. Someone who is outside the realm of normal, but can still relate to normal. Someone who knows how to be individual and powerful without bringing harm to those who want to just be predictable. Our uniqueness doesn't give us a license to be a moron; it is key to our ability to lead, transform, and create!

I've never been a follower of rules, and I never could quite handle it when so-called experts told me something was a certain way "because that's just the way it is," even if it didn't sound logical or moral. That doesn't work for me because I was created and designed for no system other than the system of my dreams. I've met a lot of you and heard similar stories from you, no matter what your income, race, gender, or other demographics might want to classify you as. You've been in my classes, and have come to my events. You write me DMs on Instagram, Facebook, and Twitter every single day. There's a fire burning inside of you, deep inside of you, in a hidden place where very few people ever get to go to. Some of you have succumbed to the pressure of normal, and now you feel as though you are dying inside. Others have given in to the pressure of rebellion, and your attempt at being individual and powerful has gotten you into trouble and drugs, and on other destructive paths. I know you, have seen you, and honestly, I understand you. There's a part of you that longs so deeply to be free that you'd give anything to have a breakthrough. Let me share with you what has helped me the most. While it might not be the path that you take, let it provoke you to create one that will be your own.

Let me share with you what has helped me the most. While it might not be the path that you take, let it provoke you to create one that will be your own.

It's not a conventional way of looking at things, by any means. To be honest with you, the minute I mention what this is, some very religious-minded people who are used to systems that explain away anything spiritual will tell me to stay on topic, get back to business, and leave that part out. *But I can't.* It's one of the anomaly sides of me that has separated me from everyone else in the business world, and it separates me from nearly everyone in the church world as well. It's my belief that getting into agreement with heaven is the answer. In heaven, I see everything as perfect, well, able, and powerful! Our answers are there! Our ideas originate there, and our power can be connected with this realm as well.

Heaven doesn't have a system, and everything created by Papa is truly unique. My business acumen in the world isn't what draws people to me to ask for strategic steps in their company. That's not what set me apart. Rather, it is my business track record and knowledge *plus* my beliefs about heaven that I am unashamed of that got me recognized and followed by millions of people. The unique way I write sales copy, and that I *pray* before I write such copy—and I mean I pray WITH the client—makes me unique. Ironically, it wasn't a hungry world or my followers who opposed me, but the traditional religious community who said I can't do that in business, and the traditional business community who said the same. But my friends, I did. Making millions of dollars didn't deter me from bringing angels, Papa, Holy Spirit, and Jesus to work with me. It doesn't mean I need you all to believe like I do or that there's a hidden agenda to this book. It means that YOU deserve to be free as well in your spiritual beliefs, even if it means you'll choose to be an atheist. You deserve to be able to live out your beliefs at work, in harmony with others!

The greatest gift Papa God ever gave to the world *was not salvation, it was FREE WILL.* You have a choice; so do I. We're not puppets. We can choose. For me? I choose heaven and all that the Bible teaches. You were given free will to choose for yourself. This is not an evangelistic book where I'm trying to change you to be like me, or I'm trying to build a parachurch organization. Far from it. But sadly, that's what the world has thought! I've sat on these two foundations my entire career, while making millions of dollars and helping others to do the same. God and business—it's normal for me. It might not be for you, but I suspect there's something buried deep inside of you that cries to be free. You might find heaven in the process of finding who you are, or you might not. My goal is that you REMEMBER who you are, and that you'll unlock the enormous potential and power you have been given.

Imagine a choir all singing the same exact melody. It's nice. But allow them to harmonize, to each bring their own unique voice *together*—that's where the magic is. We too are magical when we are allowed to share our uniqueness. Our beautiful diversity, when brought together in harmony, brings us to a higher place of unity than we could ever get to alone. We spend more hours in the workplace than we do any other place in our lives. We spend more time with the people we work with than even the people we say are our highest priority! My big question becomes this: If we are wired with a specific calling and gift, and we're told at work that we can't bring the spiritual into that place, are we truly, really, fully awake and alive in our work? I don't think so. But this doesn't mean we're setting up parachurch organizations in the marketplace. Sigh. That's the conclusion where most people will go to. Why? Because it's all we've known. It's time to pioneer a new movement, a new system without walls, and a new dimension that's been waiting to be born.

When I realized I was created for passion with all of my outside-the-box ways of creating things, seeing things, and even living, it was an exhilarating and terrifying revelation. When you're terrified and excited at the same time, you're really onto something! I believe this with my whole heart. Excited to move forward but terrified of what people will think; excited to see the things we are creating in our heads come to life but also terrified that we aren't strong enough for the task. This is where I have found a need for MORE. Being an anomaly is that more: the deviated, broken, out-of-the-box way of doing things, that invites in its own unique way all the angels, muses, helpers, and spiritual insights we could ever need to play along.

I knew that Papa had made me to be passionate—full of passion about a lot of things. But this revelation didn't make me happy or secure. Not everyone likes passion. Some people are threatened by it. But my DNA was wired for a challenge. If I'm not chasing a challenge at work, finding new ways to write ads, figuring out how to lower our budget, or using new words to get a response in my marketing, I'm already dying. To keep me thriving, healthy, and filled with the most energy possible, I must find a target and go after it with all that I am. *And* I need to go outside the bounds of the typical. Many of my clients have called me a "mad scientist of marketing" because I'll just change things a little, tweak this, edit that, and adjust this . . . and WAIT for something to explode. It's like a scientist who has 100 beakers on his table, and he's adding just a 1 to 2 percent variable in the alterations. Then he sits, waits, and watches. I do this myself with my work. But if I don't go all in, with everything I have, it's just not enough. Ninety-nine percent is failure when it comes to effort. I have to go at it with all that I am or just go home.

I've identified what holds me back and what propels me forward. I'm eager to show you how to do the same on the pages of this book. Being able to have times in my work when I can lock myself up in my office and create while taking breaks to dance, sing, and just be myself has led to some of my best work. If you sat outside the room while I'm writing this, you'd hear absolute silence at times and other times, music so loud you might not be able to think. I may be dancing during some of the process, or lying on the floor praying, waiting for Papa to expand my mind so that I can find the answer.

As many of you have probably experienced, my old way of handling my uniqueness and the opposition that can come in life led me to just stop answering, and shutting off at times. Then it led me to fighting back constantly, trying to explain *everything to everyone*, believing that somehow this would stop the friction. But it never did. Brave communication means that I had to learn to communicate bravely, and keep a safe space open for communication with other people too. If hard things needed to be discussed, I couldn't bring in accusations, suspicion, or blame. None of these things were going to serve me, and they won't serve you either. We can say how we're feeling or what might be triggering us without having to find someone or something to blame. When we take off our need to blame and put on bravery, we open a door that allows all of us to speak and communicate. Imagine being able to do this in our work! It will require love to win, always. We must love even if we disagree; we have to be willing to love, even if we don't understand. Bringing love into the workplace is quite the anomaly concept—but if we don't love in all that we do, we'll just end up with what we currently have. It's time for a change.

We've got to fly! It's how Papa made us, and it's our destiny. A big key to living a vibrant, powerful life is understanding how you were made and being willing to grow and heal so that you can become fully that, and not something someone else decided to cut out of a box for you to become. It's not an easy journey, but it is one worth pursuing relentlessly! If YOU don't write your story, someone else will. You'll wake up one day talking about your history, and you will see that you didn't create any of it. OR you can wake up one day and tell the history that you wrote and created. It's up to you!

When you understand who you are, what you were made for, how you are wired, and why that struggle inside of you *is revealing so much of the path that leads to your destiny*, you'll find that pleasing other people becomes irrelevant. Healing will be easier, living in your truest whole state will be easier, and taking on the challenges of day-to-day living will also be easier.

What is that you say? You've tried this before and took all of the designed-for-success tests and you're still confused?

Great. I was there too. So I truly get it.

As I give you some journal starters and activation exercises throughout this book, it's my prayer that they will cause you to think differently and to see things in a way that are aligned perfectly for you.

When I took personality, character trait, and career assessment tests, the more information I got about how I was created, the more confused I became as to what my day-to-day life should look like as I chased my dreams. But when I discovered that even the choices I was making, how I made them, and how little things that most tests and people ignore revealed critical information about my uniqueness, it became clear that I was on to something. *That something, if you will, is what this book is about.*

I'll walk you through a process that will help you find all that you've been looking for. While some of what I say on this journey may seem like things you've already heard or done, let me assure you that at the end of our time together, when you finish this book and get ready to set it aside, your life will be different. I'm going to provoke you to think, see, and be different. I will help you see that you have been uniquely designed and that your pursuit of "fitting in" is the enemy.

I will help you see that you have been uniquely designed and that your pursuit of "fitting in" is the enemy.

MY ROAD TO RICHES WAS THE ROAD LESS TRAVELED

My dream and finding my truest self didn't happen because a millionaire mentored me. It wasn't possible because there were business partners gathered around me in a boardroom helping me to make the best decisions for my future. No. Guesswork, risk taking, and being willing to act on my hunches were something I had to learn, a process that was oftentimes very, very painful. When we have to take risks and guess our way into the future, the people around us who may be more used to calculated efforts and strategic, so-called planning may think we're irresponsible or even irrational. But for me, it paid off in a big way. I would later discover that this is exactly how I am wired—how I was designed for success. Being able to share these experiences with my mastermind clients has helped to unlock many doors for them as well, in their careers, their relationships, and their personal lives.

Calculated efforts are important, and making sure things are mapped and planned out has its place. But for me, the visionary and anomaly that I am, jumping before I even knew if I could make it was a big key to my success. It was a lonely journey, for sure. But when you take a different path from most people, you have unique experiences, which often lead to *unique insights*.

The road less traveled has its own rewards.

And it was worth every struggle I had to go through, because now I can help you to get to where you're supposed to be as well, and it won't be guesswork. It will be like a divinely laid-out map that your heart and spirit have longed to follow your entire life. If you're a planning-type person who is strategic in everything you do, that's great! For you to be like me would be detrimental to both of us. We need each other and we need for each of us to embrace who we were created to be.

My path to being an entrepreneur and eventually making millions of dollars started when the dot-com bust was taking place and people were leaving Internet startups. Yes, this is when I started my very first online business. One of my greatest strengths in life and business is the ability to go in the *opposite direction of the masses* when I see trends and patterns forming. I could see a trend happening in my own life. And I began to pursue it with all that was within me. But I was oblivious to any news of a bust taking place online with Internet businesses. You see I had no clue what any of that was or that it was even taking place. In my sheltered life of homeschooling and raising little boys, a dream was growing inside of me. It wasn't a big dream so to speak, but it would reveal a lot about my true nature and how I was going to achieve success.

So, pay attention to the little things you do over and over again. If you find that you tend to go in the opposite direction that most people do, ask yourself why. Is it because it's easier? Does it feel more natural to you to do things contrary to the way others do them? Are you avoiding the crowd or are you creating a new path, or maybe both? You could find that this tendency opens up a whole new way of seeing things, if you let it. Go there. It could be something that other people even criticize and judge about you, so be cautious about overlooking or dismissing things that you currently believe are your negatives. For example, the person who has been called a control freak or obsessive about house cleaning could have an innate ability to set things in order, bring peace to chaos, and to make things pretty, again. This can be used in a variety of scenarios in business from housecleaning to leadership to project management! These so-called negatives that you keep doing or ending up in could be key facets of your DNA that need to be sharpened, reinvented, and used powerfully.

For me, the tendency that I've had to not need other people's input, to go on my own and reinvent and customize how I do things so that I can get on the fastest road to the result ended up being the skill sets and habits I bring to my business, the very same traits that have caused people to call me a pioneer. I never intended to pioneer anything! I didn't even care about "starting new ways" of doing things. To me the traditional way seemed way too laborious and boring, so I did it my way. I didn't set out to pioneer a movement where spirituality was welcomed in the boardroom without making it a parachurch organization, but the people who follow me and buy our products say that's the reason they love to work with me! Even those who have beliefs very different than mine say that by seeing me be my authentic self in business, they felt motivated to do the same. They just want to be fully awake, alive, and living in all they've been given.

THERE'S ALWAYS A SOLUTION

My dream in the 1990s was a $900 kitchen mixer. My reality was a household income that was much less than that. Now pay attention. The first thing my brain began to process was the profit per mixer and how I could get one for free if I sold a few. My brain didn't think about how I was going to sell them, get distributor rights for selling them, or even who I was going to sell them to. No, the "solutionist" in me saw the big picture and backtracked through the details as necessary. If the profit was $90 per mixer sold retail, or $250 per mixer kit complete with everything you need per unit sold, then my goal would be to sell enough so that I could turn around and get one myself. Simple. Well, in my head it was. And I did just that. But in retrospect I'm absolutely fascinated by my innate ability to see a business plan before I even owned my first online business. The "easy math" in my mind was not so easy for a lot of people trying to do the same thing. My natural tendency was to keep it simple, find the fastest road, and get my cotton pickin' mixer!

The big "WHY" fueling my dream was not financial freedom, a life that I could do anything I wanted in, or even building a destiny that my children would later stand on and call the starting point to all of their dreams coming true. No. I was making bread from scratch and was frustrated that every time I made a loaf, it was gone in less than 30 minutes. Three hungry boys and a husband devoured my masterpiece faster than I could say, "Did you enjoy that?" Something had to give. My strategist mind kicked in immediately. I ran to the Internet and began to search out ways to make large quantities of dough in my home kitchen so that I could make 10 loaves at a time. Here's another one of those "take note" sections that I really need *you* to take note of. Ready? Here goes: no one in my life and circle of friends and family were making 10 loaves of bread at a time. As a matter of fact, the people who knew I was making bread from scratch for my family thought it was a cute *Little House on the Prairie*–type thing and would quickly pass and be put aside as I chased a new passion. But that's not how my passion hunting worked! I either jumped all the way in or I didn't jump at all. So, now that I've built multimillion-dollar companies over and over again, using my anomalous way of thinking and being, when students in my classes ask me if I think they can do what they are attempting to do in their own small businesses, and they tell me that no one they know is doing this—like the girl who doesn't want to start a brick-and-mortar soap and lotion store but wants to do it only online or the man who has a dream of building a company who is horrible at math but has an innate heaven-given gift to bring people together and to help heal relationships—and that most of the people in their life think they're crazy for even attempting it, I reassure them that this is a perfect place to be. It's oftentimes where destiny is created! *Note:* My desire for making more bread dough in one setting would lead me to making my first million dollars in business. You have no idea where you'll end up if you chase your dreams and make a commitment to never fit in again.

One of my students, whom I'll call Erika, is in a direct sales company that makes stamping products. She didn't want to do face-to-face parties and regular local sales, though. Her dream office is a crafting space her hubby and she created where every-thing she needs is in one place. She loves to create, design, and even teach in that space. It's her favorite thinking space. But she wants to do it on her own timeline. She didn't want to leave her home but wanted to be able to build a successful business. She hates being in front of the camera, but really needed to be able to show people how to do what she's become known for! So we created a few courses she could teach online, and I helped her to use her unique ability to communicate how simple things were to do on a Facebook page. When it became absolutely necessary for her to "show and tell" this process, we created a way where she can set up her "video studio" and only show her hands and the products she's using. Her voice is amazing and personal, so it wasn't necessary to show her face. I could have tried to con-vince her over and over again how personable and inviting she looks when you look into her eyes, but she wanted *none* of that. So . . . we studied hand models, how people show their rings and bracelets online without ever showing their faces. She trained her voice and practiced cadence, and we figured out how she could lead with all of her gifts but only have her face on her website and Facebook page in the profile section, not live in videos.

When she launched her first course she sold more than she had ever done before—not only of the courses, but the back-end stamping products as well! She was thrilled because she had done the entire filming in sweatpants, a nice shirt, and no makeup. All you could see was her great shirt and her beautiful hands, with her inviting and reassuring voice leading the way. It was a home run! So much so that when she began to come out from behind the screen onto the camera, she found all of her gifts and talents awaiting her. Here was a woman who did NOT want to be filmed—someone very talented and a true anomaly in her own right who didn't want to do things like everyone else. If I hadn't helped her to reinvent the typical process of market-ing and selling these products, she probably wouldn't have more than 80,000 people interacting with her page every day or a big successful business.

I'VE GOT TO HAVE FAITH

As you read this, it is no doubt obvious to you that I am a person of faith. It may also be surprising to you that I share it so openly. Faith and success in business are usually seen as separate entities, never to come together. People work really hard to separate the spiritual and the secular. At work we want to use all that we've been given, which includes bringing our spirit, mind, body, and soul with us to our projects. If we take out the spiritual, we're all losing. But this doesn't mean we're trying to convert everyone to believe as we do, be like us, or to go to the place of worship we might go to! It simply means we want to live fully awake, alive, and be at our best at work and invite others to do the same. The truth is, bringing faith into my work is one of the ways in which I express my anomaly identity. It is simply me being me. And faith is my secret weapon when fighting resistance.

When I first started building my business 23 years ago, it was completely natural to me to bring Papa into my work. Being a person of faith is a part of who I am, who I have always been, and now it's one of the things that sets me apart from many other successful business and marketing experts. I can't imagine success without Papa God. Because for me, partnering with God, and welcoming the Holy Spirit into my business every single day, is one of the keys to being so successful.

Bringing the spiritual to work every day, however, has never meant that I try to convert others around me to embrace the same faith I hold dear. No. It simply means that I want to be all that I'm meant to be—and what Papa has created me to be, with my spirit wide open—and I'm committed to bringing that into both my personal and business relationships.

Initially, the churches that I went to didn't understand me and wanted to change me. It didn't matter if I went to a conservative, charismatic, new age, or even universal-type church! The same power that I had to influence large groups of people was a threat to those who had to have "their way" no matter how liberal or open-minded they thought they were. It was the same in the business world. In the religious world I was judged for talking about money too much. Those in the business world viewed me with skepticism because I talked about God too much. But all that felt foreign and limiting to me because I don't believe you can have too much money, and I don't believe you can have too much God. Being on the receiving end of so much judgment from both sides helped me realize that I was somewhat of an anomaly in both worlds. For me to be recognized and to succeed in both realms, I'd have to reinvent how things were done.

So that's what I did.

I'll give you an example: As a business and marketing expert, it's not uncommon for me to do a live conference or webinar where I'll share my vast experience and knowledge of copywriting, direct response marketing, pay-per-click ads, and the like. But at the end of the class I'll release a blessing over my attendees, unashamedly, reminding them that I didn't get here alone and that bringing their spiritual beliefs into their work could give them the same edge. When I speak or preach at a church, it's not unusual for me to use data, charts, and graphs, showing percentages that reveal why the church is missing the mark by gathering in their local buildings and ignoring—or worse yet, judging—the world we live in.

Both of my worlds mesh very well. But it took quite a "move of God" if you will, to get people to see it from my perspective. Social media opened the gates. In social media the voice of every person in the world is important and can be heard. Facebook, Twitter, and Instagram gave everyone a voice. We can now connect with nearly anyone we want to. What most people don't see is that the gate to the spiritual in our world has also opened in a big way!

For many of us, the concept of work means endurance. We endure our work, we work hard and put our heads down for years trying to achieve our dreams, being sold the notion that once we lift our head up and can retire, we'll really be living. That concept made me cringe. No, it was stronger than that. It made me furious! This was not what I wanted for my life, and hundreds of thousands of clients in my classrooms have told me the same. They want to enjoy their work and they want to be fulfilled in the work that they do. How can this ever be possible if we keep separating the spiritual and secular, and how can we ever be fully awake and alive when we're leaving the spiritual for only Sunday mornings? I answered this question by bringing both with me everywhere, and ironically it attracted millions of people on social media who want to do the same!

TWO HALVES DON'T MAKE A WHOLE

We are anomalies, all of us. And for many of us, part of not fitting in is that we can't seem to separate our spiritual self from our professional self. And you know what? We shouldn't. For others it's your unique way of seeing things that has caused you trouble, because when you buck the system with your opinions, you're met with opposition that causes fear. Still others of you have a very unconventional way of getting things done that might look like the polar opposite of how others typically do it. All of these things will fuel your beliefs, your mannerisms, and even your worldview.

It's important to know that our beliefs fuel everything we do. From a purely neurological standpoint, human beings never even act on anything, nor do we even get a desire to act on anything, without first having a thought and a belief to do something. As beings with a body, soul, and spirit, these three components of our humanness are inseparable. But sadly, in the industries most of us work in, we are being asked to behave as if this wasn't the case.

Everything I have done to build a very successful brand that has helped and is helping tens of thousands of small business owners and even several large corporations, is being driven by my spiritual and anomalous worldview—that people have intrinsic value and are worth paying attention to, that heaven is interested in all that we do, and, ultimately, that breaking the rules isn't always a path to destruction but can be the initiation of transformation and higher levels of success.

Believe me, I understand that the mom and pop just beginning their entrepreneurial journey and the multibillionaire with thousands of staff all fight the war of fear, doubt, and discourage-ment. No one has ever gotten to a place of influence and success without first walking through a lot of criticism, self-doubt, fear, and even insecurity. Especially for those of us who are anom-alies, who think differently, act differently, and succeed differ-ently. But succeed, we do. Probably because we are different. And "different" is good. In fact, that's exactly what has happened to me. And it is possible for you too.

That's why I wrote this book.

This is not just about my personal journey from homeschool-ing mother of three to millionaire by age 30. It's about all of us who have never felt like we fit in yet ultimately know that limit-less possibilities exist in each of us.

In business, the way to have success is not so much in being alike, as every other retailer, manufacturer, or developer on the planet. But rather it's taking something that has multiple variet-ies in the marketplace and meeting a need in such a way that no one even wants to look at your competition.

Steve Jobs was the master at this. Napster had already cre-ated a music-streaming service, but Steve put that music in your pocket! Today, if a phone is even going to sell, this feature is stan-dard. When he initiated this anomalous move, they thought he was crazy.

You don't fit in. You stand out because you're pioneering your way right to where your customer needs you the most. To get really powerful is to get really masterful at one thing. If you are serious about seeing success in your life and your business, become good at one very unique "never-fitting-in" thing—then no one can touch you. And as you master this thing, I want to encourage you to reach deep. Go into the deep end, which might include the spiritual as it has for me. Or it might mean initiating something that has never been done before that seems easy for you but that people say is absolutely unheard of and impossible. I'll never forget the reaction that Steve Jobs, anomalous leader and wonder of my generation, heard about the iPad in its first creative days. "You can't make that happen, you'd have to sand-paper people's fingers down to make it work." Today, the iPad leads the trail as one of the top most successful products ever created. Do you think Steve had to think differently to cause this success? You bet he did! I bet if we could see it now, we'd see angels, partners, and worlds unknown cheering him on when he felt most alone. I bet we'd see geniuses that had gone before him and of whom the world was not worthy cheering him on in the spiritual realm, fanning his flame late at night when he wanted to give up. Imagine for just one minute that you too have such a cheerleading squad around you. Where could you go if that were true? I believe it is.

CONTROL YOUR THOUGHTS OR YOUR THOUGHTS WILL CONTROL YOU

In order to build a business and to become all that you were designed to be, you must break free from the cycle of poverty that dominates and controls so many people. Limited thinking that expects the worst won't make your dreams come true. It won't release the fresh breath of wisdom and life into the projects you're working on. Sadly, many of you have been groomed to expect lack. How many times have you asked yourself *What if it does work out?* rather than *What if it doesn't?* What if all those dreams you've had actually start to come true and things start going your way? What if the reason you can't let go of your dreams is because you are supposed to change the world with them? My friend, I need to warn you—it's a WAR. A real war, this battle for the life you were meant to live and the life you're currently living. And it is my belief and experience that one of our greatest barriers to success is our tendency to prepare for failure. We try to protect ourselves from disappointment and to avoid expecting too much out of life. We put up all kinds of protection around us: financial protection, reputation protection, and self-protection. Do you realize what an insult that is to Papa God and to the entire world? When we try to calculate how we are going to do what we were made to do, we are not really believing in possibility, our dreams coming true, and the power of being an anomaly. We are living in poverty, lack, and struggle.

The power of expectation is incredible. Our brain was made for it. Scientists say that when we live in happiness and expectation we open up areas of our brain that are completely locked when we live in doubt and fear. Expectation is something that I believe has been woven into our very being and DNA. The power of expectation is a gift from heaven. It is hope, the promise, the faith we need to change our world and to create a better future for all anomalies that come after us.

Expectation is a double-edged sword. We can expect success or we can expect failure with the same gifts and abilities. The very same power it takes to see what is in your head come to life can be used to destroy what is in front of you and shut off the possibility in your mind. At the end of the day, we must guard our thoughts, make them obey our goals, and learn to fight our own war. Think about it: Children do not expect that Santa Claus will disappoint them until some cantankerous adult who is stricken with skepticism starts to shoot down their dreams. They lay out cookies! They believe! I remember believing that I heard footsteps and the *crash* when he came down the chimney. My level of expectation and belief has always been very high. It's why when I wasn't careful, I could believe myself straight into a hellish pit of death and suffering.

We are programmed to think we can't afford things—it's too hard, we can't possibly do such-and-such because people like us just don't do such things. We can even be told we're not made for such things, we aren't able, we shouldn't, and we'll get into trouble if we even attempt to do something different! When you set out to change your life—whether it's starting a business, wanting to lose weight, breaking an addiction, crushing gender stereotypes, or anything that goes beyond what your family and friends are doing—you will see how deeply any poverty mind-sets have lodged themselves into your beliefs, and ultimately, your DNA.

As I lead my students in my Inner Circle mastermind and Small Business academy every week, one of the most common reasons people give for not being able to start their businesses is a lack of money. I've trained them that money isn't what we lack—it's knowledge. Money is easy to find when we have the knowledge we need. Getting things to come together is simple when we have the knowledge to do so. But kicking ourselves in our own butt every day that we don't "feel like it" because our own stinking thinking gets in the way is the real war.

The truth is I was massively in debt when I built my first business. This was not an excuse I used to hold me back. But I hear this excuse every single day. The real issue is this: these students lack *knowledge*, not money—knowledge of how to make something out of nothing, how to flip things they have for a profit so that they can get what they want, and how to go without for a while so that they can get to a place where they can have anything they want. It takes risk, massive amounts of risk. This is not an "I'll try this on a weekend and see if it works, and if not, I'll just go back to the job I hate on Monday" mentality. No, it's more like, "I cannot and will not live like this any longer, and I will do anything I have to do to make this dream come true!" I sold things that I had, even things that were important to me. That's risky! But there was no way I was going to stay where I was.

There's a reason for the journey, and there's purpose in the things you'll learn. Not everything in life comes easy or naturally. Some of the best things in life happen when you feel like you're getting nowhere—and then you wake up one day to realize you have pushed through your fears, your worries, and the judgments and negative words of others, and you are where you were designed to be. Everything Papa had hidden from you *is now your life.*

BIG-PICTURE LESSON

Not fitting in has always had negative connotations in our society. It seemed like being different was the enemy to winning in life. But the trouble is, those of us who are different have wasted far too much time and energy pushing ourselves to fit into a mold that constrains our creativity, intelligence, and perspective. The square peg will never fit into the round hole, after all. But why should it? The message—I should say, the false message—is that if we were just like everyone else, we'd finally achieve our goals and have peace, right? But the key to inner peace and reaching our potential is actually in celebrating *not* fitting in. How glorious is that? Because when you think about it, the very idea of trying to "fit in" is about conforming into a preexisting structure. It's limited and limiting. And by the way, it's the structure that is shaped in a way that doesn't fit *us*—not the other way around. Why don't we ever look at it from that perspective? Wouldn't that change everything? It would. I believe it's because heaven has made us extraordinarily powerful. When we realize this, embrace it, and live it, we are truly limitless.

ANOMALY ACTION: WHAT IS LIFE TEACHING YOU AND HOW CAN YOU LISTEN TO YOUR JOURNEY SO FAR?

Take this quiz to see if you can find lessons and clues that are signposts that you were created for something unique and much more than the state you currently are living in.

1. ☐ ☐ As a child, did you question rules that
   YES NO didn't make sense to you, but ultimately were pressured or forced into abiding them? Or did you give in because it's what all the other kids were doing?

2. ☐ ☐ Have you ever been called out or criticized
   YES NO on how you dress, what type of hairstyle you have, or your creative style? If so, did it make you feel embarrassed or ashamed in any way? Did you feel a pull to compromise as much as you felt a pull to fight back?

3. ☐ ☐ Have you ever been praised by a friend or
   YES NO family member for making "the safe or sensible choice" when in your heart, you regretted your decision? How did this pan out 10, 20, or even 30 years later?

4. ☐ ☐ Have you ever wanted to say "no" to
   YES NO something with every fiber of your being,
           only to keep quiet and go along with it so
           as not to make waves?

5. ☐ ☐ Have you ever been excessively criticized
   YES NO or even mocked after sharing your dreams
           with someone you trusted?

6. ☐ ☐ Have you ever been told, even as a child,
   YES NO to stop "pushing the envelope"?

7. ☐ ☐ Do you have friends or family members
   YES NO who often tell you what you're not, such
           as "you're not a painter," even though you
           feel called to paint?

8. ☐ ☐ Do you often feel pulled between two
   YES NO extremes? Have you ever felt a sense of
           hopelessness about your life because no
           matter how hard you tried, you
           couldn't fit in?

9. ☐ ☐ Have you ever felt like you had to
   YES NO compromise your beliefs in order to be
           accepted at work, with your family, or in
           your place of worship?

Assessment

- If you answered yes to 6 or more questions, you
  possess the qualities of an anomaly—someone who
  doesn't fit in because you are called to be different.
  This book can be a powerful resource for you as you
  seek to be truer to your nature and to realize your
  full potential.

- If your answers were fairly evenly divided between yes and no, you may be called to be a mediator. You have a type of wisdom that can be a gift to anomalies seeking their own path. As you read though this book, pledge to be honest and accepting of yourself, and to be open to seeing yourself as you were created—powerful and one who brings hope to situations.

- If you answered no to 6 or more questions, you may be an anomaly who is breaking free from past limitations. Use this book as fuel for your continued freedom. Remembering that not all anomalies are alike. Some initiate, some support, some bridge the gap, and some change everything all together for all of us.

Grab a Journal!

Right now, grab a journal and write out the first thing that comes to your mind. Do you feel like what you've learned from taking the quiz on page 26 is new information, or something you've always known? This is where we'll start our journey together. Learning to walk powerfully while not fitting in will require some daily courage, and journaling is a great way to find it. Your journal isn't a place where you share things with other people. No, it's a safe place where you take the thoughts, feelings, and dreams of your soul and write them out. No filter, no rules, just you and the paper.

RESISTANCE: THE BRICK WALL

Along the way to achieving a big dream, you will encounter opposition. Don't believe me? If your dream is to create a business that will bring in more than a million dollars a year in profit, then say that out loud. In front of other people. Tell your family. Share your goals with your closest friends. What do you think they will say? "Good for you! You've always had great potential. I'm so happy that you are on the path to success!" Heck no! Most people will tell you that you're getting too big for your britches. That your dreams are out of reach. That you are selfish to want more. That is the voice of resistance. Get to know it because it will show up at every step in your journey. It's just a fact of life that we not only have to be prepared for, we really need to stop being so shocked when it shows up. I'm right here with you, so please don't think I have all the answers. No one does. We know this is going to happen, and still when it does, it hurts, it can be confusing, and oftentimes, it can throw us off course.

Have you ever been moving toward your dream fast and then hit a brick wall of naysayers, criticism, internal duress, or even sheer terror? That happened to me. The closer I got to where I am today, someone or something reminded me to only go so far. Why do we do that to each other? Do we really think we're helping each other out? We do this to friends, family members, and even strangers on social media whom we have never even met and have no clue about! Why do we do this? Is it because we really want to help someone, or could it be that we are so disgusted with where we are in life, we set out to correct someone else, believing it will make us feel better about ourselves? It never does. So we start feeling even worse, and we do it again to someone else and we feel worse, and it's a vicious cycle!

The voice of societal resistance had been telling me to sit down, shut up, and be quiet since I was a little girl. I know the voice well. But I don't have to listen to it, and neither do you.

And there's an even bigger enemy we all face that has a louder, craftier voice that can be downright terrifying and even murderous in its assault! It's our own voice of self-judgment. The words we often speak to and about ourselves really can be the most dangerous. Forget demons in hell and haters online; we are our own worst enemies most of the time. When we set out to do something unique and powerful and to rise above fitting in, it's ironic that we don't become our own best cheerleaders.

Instead, we oftentimes become our own worst judges. For me, it was the voices of inadequacy and feeling undeserving that haunted me the most. "I didn't have what it took, never would, and no matter how hard I tried, never could." Beyond that, even if I did someday actually rise up to be equal or greater than the challenge, I wouldn't deserve to see my dreams come true. I believed at the core of who I was that I deserved to fail, struggle, and even suffer.

The voice within is echoed by the voice of resistance from your environment. It will accuse you falsely, judge you harshly, and when you finally do well, will say you didn't deserve it and aren't allowed to go forward. Believe me, I know. The religious have rebuked me, leaders have attempted to sabotage me, my own heart was against me, my family sought to hold me back, and my own mind found a comfortable, quiet place to hide. In pain.

This war comes from both you and other human beings. It's not some cosmic force or even demons from hell, as many would imply, but rather, it's that enemy of champions who fears that the light and power they were given is far too great to carry. When our destiny comes face to face with fear in others, it will require forgiveness, patience, grace, kindness, and love to be all that we're meant to be. When it cuts you deeply in the secret parts of your heart that no one has ever had access to, its poison could kill you. To protect ourselves, we must be mindful of the journey and process that it takes to actually go from where we are to where we want to be. Find new friends, create new social media profiles where you can be your truest self and attract the same. Remember, hiding in a box or boundary never created for you won't help attract the people you were meant to do life with. Be brave and find your tribe! You deserve it.

> ### Spiritual Takeaway
> Everyone is made uniquely and strategically, and today I am writing a new story for my life. I am not meant to fit in. I am meant to rise above limitations and reach my limitless potential.

CHAPTER 2

YOUR ANOMALY LINCHPIN

Fresh warm bread from the oven. The smell flooded my small home with hints of warm melted butter and fresh home-made strawberry jam. Berries I had smashed and cooked, added just the right amount of sugar so that it was a masterpiece. You'd think you had just encountered heaven with every bite. There was really nothing like it. As I stood at my kitchen sink, looking out the window at my boys playing outside on our three acres, I just knew that all of my dreams were about to come true. Warm bread can do that to you. My dreams of mothering perfection would finally be reality.

I loved cooking, creating, and showing my love for my family in the kitchen. Being resourceful and practical were also things I leaned on, so my first attempt at bringing a bit of *Little House on the Prairie* into my home was actually frozen bread dough from the local grocery store, store-bought butter, and my homemade freezer jam. I hadn't quite started to learn how to can yet, so my early years as a mommy and homemaker were spent bringing old-fashioned traditions into my home in easy, quick ways.

"Oh, Momma, this is soooooooo good! Can we have another piece? Pleeeease!" my three little guys would squeal as they bit into the little bite of heaven I had just created. But it didn't last long. Heaven on earth was quickly replaced by empty plates and full bellies. If I wanted more of this divine food encounter, I'd have to figure out how to double my results and make more than one loaf at a time. Initially I just used three frozen loaves and baked them three at once. But this got costly, and I knew that feeding my family more white bread long term was not a very healthy choice. So I went back to the woman who taught me this fine art: a soft-spoken, gentle, and beautiful woman at church named Barb who would become my personal Mothering Mentor.

My childhood home didn't include warm bread at the kitchen table every morning with giggles for breakfast. There were no memories of heaven on earth as we enjoyed dinner together at the family table. This could have made me bitter and angry. Instead, it made me want to be a perfect mom. One who would give her children everything she never had. I had prayed for Papa to bring me some women who could help me be a better wife and mother. My heart's cry was to break the patterns of my childhood, and to bring my family life and joy in spite of the fact that all my memories still flashed back to sadness, pain, and loneliness.

A SPIRITUAL MENTOR

Barb was the answer to my prayers. She always wore dresses and never seemed frustrated. She had patience and love for every one of her seven children, and such warm admiration for her husband. So she became my role model in my late 30s, as I raised my three sons. Funny, isn't it, that I remember how her dresses and her lack of frustration were the things I desired the most? At the time, I was a young mom, living in sweatpants and complete frustration. So, she became someone I aspired to be. My mind quickly took pictures and paid attention to her mannerisms, tone, facial expressions, and the Bible verses she quoted. She was exactly what Proverbs 31 spoke of when describing a virtuous woman. I was going to become that too. My focus was fixed, and my pursuit of perfect mothering began.

Little did I know that this quest would lead me to start my very first online business and make my first million dollars. Or that along the way, I would encounter personal self-judgment at a level I never knew was possible. Perfectionism snuck into my equation for success in my personal and business life and would later become an enemy I'd fight with for many years. Though I didn't start a business around being a perfect mother, it was at the forefront of everything I did at the time. I would clean perfectly, have a sweet demeanor, have patience and love for everyone around me, make all of our food from scratch, and stay up late in the night, as the Bible said, taking care of my children and living on very little sleep, as an outpouring of my love for my family. It was also a part of my focus on being perfect. Dreams of a Christian magazine or *Better Homes & Gardens* coming and interviewing me danced in my head as I took my frozen dough out of the freezer, greased my bread pans, and made my loaves from heaven. The very thing that made me a pioneer who created new paths knew that I wanted to create something very different for my children then I had experienced as a young girl. Rather than creating something amazing, my dreams were to be better than anything I had ever seen, and my insecurities led me to perfectionism. My experience has taught me that perfection is a poor answer to insecurity. We want to be excellent and committed in the work we do. We want our lives to bring forth our very best. But perfection, flawless and without error, is impossible in this human journey. Some of the best companies come out of a big mess. Some of the best life stories come out of horrific pain. Just because there's chaos doesn't mean a message for the whole world isn't being created. Guard against perfection and pay close attention to wanting to overcompensate in areas that might need healing. Sometimes our way out can be a doorway into what we're meant to do. Getting away from pain can be our out to freedom, and learning to not strive for perfection our doorway to helping others.

BREAD BUILDS A BUSINESS

As a homeschooling mom in the late 1990s, I had a simple dream. I wanted to bake fresh bread for my three sons, and I wanted to make a lot of it at one time—8 to 10 loaves, to be exact.

But I needed the right kitchenware. Being an anomaly, I didn't just go to the store and buy a bread maker off the shelves like others might have. Truth is, I couldn't afford one. But that didn't stop me. No. Instead, it drove me to research how to sell such equipment online, so it could be shipped from a huge company's warehouse. I discovered in my research that there were other moms pursuing the same idea of "perfect mothering" just like me all over the world, and companies that made kitchenware for the perfect woman's kitchen! If I sold enough bread makers and grain mills, after paying for each unit and shipping, mine could easily be purchased with the profits. So that's how my first business plan was created. Actually, I didn't even know that's what people did when they started a company: create a business plan.

When I made my first million, I was living in the middle of nowhere, in a town of less than 2,000 people. To say I was isolated is an understatement. I had no one to teach me how to be a successful businesswoman. This is why my normal way of doing things is to "ask heaven" and see what I hear. I prayed. And let me just say, I prayed about everything, like one of the biggest pests heaven has ever known!

I would pray, "Papa, give me a photographic memory so I can have pictures in my mind of all of these sales pages, websites, graphics, strategies, and . . ."

"Papa, help me to write this description."

"Holy Spirit, how do I write an e-mail that gets people to respond to me?"

"Papa, would you send angels to my pay-per-click ads and have them go further than I've even paid for?"

"Papa, can you please show me how to set my bids and what to pay so I don't lose a lot of money?"

I swear to you that these are the things I prayed about, and what I begged Papa to help me with back then humbles me now. It's also very inspiring, because after you've been doing this thing for 24 years, it's easy to get confidence in yourself and comfortable in what has always been. I'm motivated by my younger self's example to go to a new level even now by trusting my faith to guide me even more. For me it's faith in Papa God; for others it might be inspiration from nature, a muse, a past relative whose life inspires them to go further. When we find this thing, I truly believe we'll go to a new level.

I have a really good friend whose mother was his superhero. Her life was cut short by cancer. Although he was raised in a faith-based community, sadly he encountered religion just like I did. He was faced with rules, regulations, and restrictions as a basis for a relationship with Papa. But his mother inspired him more than anyone ever had, so she became his anomaly motivator. Ironically, when he heard about the title of this book, he said she used to always tell him as a young boy that he was an anomaly. He broke the mold in his life in many capacities, being a single dad, getting a master's degree, starting several businesses in very unconventional ways. While he isn't always as motivated as I am by faith and heaven, he still believes. It's just his mother was the person who gave him courage, faith, and wisdom for so many years in life. Even though she's gone, she still inspires and motivates his decisions today.

A SUPERNATURAL BUSINESS

The results of bringing the spiritual into my business were incredible. I never intended for it to be my "anomaly thing," but it became that. It was the dividing line, the separator, the thing that caused me to deviate from the typical path of direct response marketing and put me into a place of celebrity on social media. I didn't just bring the spiritual into my business, and become a faith-based company like so many others. No. That's not me. I lived my life openly, which included my deep relationship with Papa, and I held a space for others to do the same no matter what they believed. This has won me a lot of respect from people who don't believe like me, but love to see how I pioneered such a movement. One of my favorite clients is Hindu. Another is an atheist. Still another is a rabbi. Bringing the spiritual into my work opened a door for diversity to live in harmony and for me to just be myself and not have to filter, disclaimer, or edit everything I said and did.

Bringing the spiritual into things also gave me courage that it wasn't all on me, this big task of building a multimillion-dollar company *while* raising my kids *and* battling several health challenges *and* at the same time living in a very painful, lonely marriage. Not only was I never alone again, I never had to fear how to get to a certain place or worry about when things would finally come together. I got so addicted to meeting with Papa God in the morning, planning out how we'd grow my brand and impact the world, that I began to sleep less and less, and pray more and more. Life was ridiculous in my business! My sales flew past $1 million fast, and my bottom line was growing at an astounding rate. So much so, that when I look back now, I'm shocked that I didn't realize how incredibly rare this was and how very few people were getting results like this.

Each of us can bring this kind of "rare" thing into our lives if we're willing to go outside of the artificial and unspoken boundaries that people have put on us. But we have to blaze our own trails to do so, maybe without even realizing it at the time. You might be doing something one day that seems so innocent and unrelated, but it could be the very key heaven uses to propel you forward in life in a way that you couldn't even imagine if you tried. For example, maybe you're in the fitness world, and your business is unique because you don't subscribe to the typical way of building a fitness company. What if your linchpin is that you know how to use functional bodywork and weight lifting to chisel the body without having to constantly teach low carbs, keto, or the typical fads? This is how a couple that I really respect has found success. Today they can be found teaching bodybuilders and everyday fitness buffs how to eat their cake and still get ripped. It's amazing and it's definitely a pioneered movement. As a matter of fact, they refer to the whole keto, low-carb, starve-yourself world in fitness and bodybuilding as "idolatry"—a worship of the "kill yourself so you're fit" mindset. They can be seen rebuking and chastising those who lead their cult followings in nonsense teaching, as they call it, with starvation diets, measuring of body fat daily, and other extreme measures. They do this all while eating Cap'n Crunch cereal, chocolate, and wine . . . and showing their ripped abs. I'm laughing even as I write this because their work infuriates the bodybuilding community in the same way the religious community seems to hate me. While these successful people don't necessarily bring faith and the spiritual into their work, they use some words that almost sound like it, which adds another anomaly way to be unique, and I LOVE IT. You can do that too.

My first company wasn't birthed by finding my ideal client, strategizing how to develop a product everyone would want, and ending up on *Shark Tank*. I just wanted to get my kitchenware for free. Yup. My budget was smaller than my desires. So I asked all of heaven for the courage and wisdom that I lacked like I do in every other thing I want to do that seems beyond me. Where someone else might seek out a more experienced business partner, I sought Papa. Pictures began to flood my mind of how I could create something even better than what people had in their brick-and-mortar stores, and it wouldn't cost me an enormous amount of overhead.

Pictures are the way my brain communicates. It's also a part of my anomaly nature. If I don't see pictures, I have a really hard time processing things. I've been seeing pictures for as long as I can remember. My love for learning has always been ferocious, but if I can't create a picture or if one doesn't come into my mind, it's hard for me to get excited about something. Pictures began to go through my head rapidly. I didn't have to be like other people. I didn't have to operate my company like others. I could do what I wanted to do! I could do all of this from my kitchen table—my used, beaten up, where we "did life" kitchen table! These humble beginnings were my launch pad to building my first seven-figure business. While I knew I was running this new company I created, I didn't quite realize at the time that I was just beginning to build something much bigger, for me, for my family, and for the millions of people I would influence years later.

As I brought the spiritual into everything I did, my heart's desires began to steer me to my destiny. Papa God wasn't asking me to sell all that I had, give up everything that was important to me, live a miserable life, and follow Him. I sought Papa, asked for help, my desires to be successful grew, and the more successful I got, the more I sought Him! Now that's a sermon that needs to be preached, wouldn't you say?

Far too often we're told that to pursue our dreams, become hugely successful, make a lot of money, and create an amazing life is in conflict with the will of God for our lives. Some call it being greedy, and write condemning sermons that they preach from dull, dry pulpits to people who are terrified of doing anything more with their lives. Others call it the lust of the flesh, stating that the desires of our heart are evil, so it goes without saying that to pursue these desires just means you're "feeding your flesh" and are not pleasing Papa. But this isn't the truth that I discovered as I built my first empire. I found Papa, and all of heaven, and the love I had longed for most of my life, while building my company and chasing my dreams. Papa God, as I like to call him, became and still is my best Friend, my Confidant, the One who can talk to me when I won't let others in, the One who helps me see wisdom when my heart races and wants to defend itself. He's my Everything.

So it makes sense that prayer, or quite frankly, just talking to Him all day, was the pillar around which I built my companies. I prayed about everything! I asked, I screamed, I got mad, I begged, and I began to feel all the emotions and struggles that were trapped inside of me from childhood through my communication with Papa.

"Papa, help me to write better ads."

"Papa, please help us to sell 10 mixers today!"

"Give us better wholesale prices."

"Make our ads go where we didn't pay for them and have our paid-for ads be at a price that is so low, even my competitors' benefit."

The things I asked Papa for were not typical, not traditional, and believe me, if anyone saw me dancing before Papa in my little home office, thanking Him for the day and believing that my joyful dance moved heaven, they would never have believed me. It's really fun now, on this side of huge success to say, "Yeah, I pretty much learned business by following my gut and asking all of heaven for help!" But back then, not so much.

A SPIRITUAL UNICORN IN BUSINESS

I've been asked a lot how I ever "got away with" bringing Papa God into everything like I do. People often refer to me as the "Spiritual Unicorn." As if it was against some criminal anti-faith business policy I didn't know about. For me it's always been natural to ask heaven about everything. This is how I learned mothering, and how to grow in discerning things, so it only made sense to apply it to my business. Bringing faith into my business was my main anomaly linchpin, and it gave me courage to just be my complete anomaly self in all that I did.

There were so many days as a young entrepreneur, just trying to make an income, that I felt overwhelmed, like I was not good enough or smart enough. The struggle to fit into this lifestyle of owning my own business didn't even seem real. I wasn't always confident when people would ask me how things were going, *but there was a constant pull in my gut to move ahead and to keep moving forward*, even if it was nowhere near perfect. This is one of the key lessons that I teach my clients today. I'll pull up my very first website through an archive tool online and show them where I was then and where I am now. Nothing was EVER perfect. They try to chase perfection and be like some expert marketer they're following online, but when I was in their shoes just starting out, I was far from perfect, and I was making hundreds of thousands of dollars in sales! Wild, isn't it? I demanded perfection of myself in other areas of my life, but one of my greatest expressions of my anomaly self came through by not trying to be perfect in my marketing or sales campaigns.

In fact, I still remember my first website like it was yester-day. It was in the late '90s when thoughts of a "search engine" were just beginning. Overture was the dominant tool we used in those days. And Majordomo was the name of the only e-mail program we had. Let me expand for you what Majordomo was and how far removed my starting point was to where small business owners begin today. When we sent out an e-mail through this program, someone had to send an e-mail to our domain (i.e., "domo"), and the responding server would then send the person an automated signal back to see if it was really him or her. Then the person would have to reply back and say it was, and the server would then ask if they wanted daily, weekly, or monthly summaries. They would have to then respond back again, and they would now be on your server list, so you could e-mail them. Like I said, this was FAR removed from the easy opt-in forms we have today and the automated systems we have that are like having a real person respond. Majordomo was as big of a deal as artificial intelligence is today, yet, as we look back on how it operated, it's quite shocking to see how anyone could have been able to successfully run a business that way. Let's face it—that's a 4-step process to get someone's e-mail! Heck, we have deliverability issues in today's world of social media and smartphones just getting people to reply to our opt-in response! We've come a long way, that is for sure, and this is why I'm so passionate about helping others to see that there's never been a better time to not only start their own business, but also to step into the independence it provides.

Don't even get me started on search engines. OMG, we had one or two back then like Lycos, and they were very popular. Then there was WebCrawler. And then the GIANT was born: Google! Little did I know then two Stanford students would ultimately create the company that would change the course of my business—and millions of other businesses in the years to come—through the power of the search engine! I was one of the first 1,000 people to sign up with Google, and these days when I call about our account, they tell me it's called a "remnant account." I've been doing this for so long I'm now a remnant! Google has been a model worthy of following. More than 20 years later, I have a habit of always watching what Google is doing, and following in some capacity.

As I look back on my first year, it's astounding to me that the ugly website with my warm face and invitation actually brought in just under $30,000 in profit. And then my first million was made the year after. In the middle of what would later be referred to as the dot-com crash, I was exploding while others were imploding. But my approach was so far out in left field, that if anyone had any clue how I was actually doing this, I wasn't sure they'd believe me or even understand my strategy. So I started to doubt myself. I started to believe a story about myself that I wasn't good enough, that my success wouldn't last, that I would get exposed as someone who didn't know what she was doing. An imposter. This voice of "fraud" began to grow louder and louder. Ironically, over the years, as I've coached hundreds of thousands of small business owners, it has become quite clear that this voice of so-called fraud is actually evidence, most times, of something that should be pursued. It's an illegitimate voice that doesn't bring any valid insight or help.

It's the voice of fear, or what I like to refer to as the "fraud police," and I started listening to it.

PARTNERING WITH HEAVEN

I didn't realize at the time that asking for help is a sign of power, not weakness. Many times when we are learning something new, we'll try to pretend like we already know things we simply do not. I've done it; I'm sure you've probably done it too. No judgment. However, one of the key breakthroughs that happened in my business career is when I started asking for help, from people and the spiritual realm. I like to teach my students how to discern just WHO they should ask for help and why it matters. For example, we don't ask our relatives and friends for business advice if they've never run a business. We don't ask for marketing advice from someone who has never done a day of marketing in their life. This should be common sense, but it simply is not. So many people are trying to "fake it till they make it," and good old-fashioned values of integrity have begun to vanish. Sadly, we live in a society that values perfection, workaholism, and independence. We aren't taught things like community or humility. As I read books as a young homemaker and business owner about powerful people who changed the world, I began to see a common thread. They asked God for help, especially when people failed or were unable to solve a serious crisis. George Mueller fed orphans with prayer. He never once asked for money. He believed that to do so was a lack of faith. No, he took all of his requests to Papa and miraculous things happened! Amy Carmichael rescued little girls out of human trafficking. She ended up mothering more than 300 little ones, and had no one to help her accomplish her goal in the capacity that she was called to. Her typical plan was to ask Papa God for help and to see mysterious and often angelic-like help manifest itself on behalf of her babies. It only made sense to me that if I wanted to do big, supernatural, impossible things in my business, asking Papa for help was the solution. I'd later hear stories of RG LaTourneau who created the first "earth mover" and became a competitor of all of the top industrial heavy-duty machinery by bringing God into his companies in the early 1900s. Matt McPherson, who owns the Mathews Bow and McPherson Guitar companies, has a similar story. Today, Mathews Inc. is the largest archery manufacturing company in the world. The development of this company came because a man listened to "promptings" and "visions" from God that came in numerical patterns and drawings of bows. Long before I heard of these two giants in business working with heaven, I was doing the same on my acreage in a tiny town in Michigan.

We're taught that God is only interested in the spiritual, and it might seem odd to bring Him into something like business, which appears secular, especially because money and sales are involved. But this doesn't make sense to me, and it doesn't align with the stories we see playing out in the Bible, either. Heaven is involved in everything. Jesus goes everywhere the religious don't want to go to. The religious world has its rules and its systems. When I began to write this book, a lot of well-meaning people tried to convince me to just keep this a business book. To leave all this "religious stuff" out. Little did they know I've been fighting that battle since day one and it's actually WHY I am writing this book and WHY this publisher wanted to take the risk to pioneer such a message: that the spiritual and secular do not have to be separated. Just because I mention God in a business book, it doesn't mean it's religious by its very nature. To separate the sacred from the secular is a disservice, as it puts heaven and Papa God into a place of disinterest when it comes to the everyday affairs of our lives. We spend more time with our co-workers than we do with anyone else, every single week. If Papa God didn't care about this part of our life, He would have to be portrayed as a distant, uncaring, unloving father who only does his duties on weekends. This is not who I know. He's interested in everything and eager to hear all about it!

Being willing to bring the spiritual into our work opens a universe of possibilities and options for us that we simply are not seeing otherwise. It's another dimension. Think about it. If Papa God and the universe that He runs know more about every aspect, perspective, insight, and opportunity available regarding every single topic we could ever address, why wouldn't we invite Him into what we do in our work? It takes faith, yes. But not giant moving, Hercules-style faith that very few of us have. No, it's childlike faith to simply acknowledge that we need help from someone or something greater than ourselves, greater than our perspective and experience.

So, is asking Papa God to help us write better Facebook ads, or to come up with ways that we can connect with people all over the world on Instagram, out of place? It's not, if you allow your faith to take you there. This has led me to also believe that it's not any more sacred or holy of an act to go feed orphans in a foreign country than it is to create an exceptional product in the marketplace and deliver it to your customers with incredible, "loving our customers" service. But to go outside the boundaries of even typical customer service, we have to be willing to believe that things can always get better. We can always do more and we can always make a difference if we allow Papa God to enter into our daily routine and lives.

BIG-PICTURE LESSON

Getting into agreement with heaven is the launchpad to a life and career that is limitless. But I'm sure this is for many of you the first time you've ever heard anyone give that kind of message who has had the kind of success I have and continue to have in my companies. Usually you're hearing this from a pulpit, from a religious leader or someone who is trying to turn the marketplace into a parachurch structure. That is NOT my goal nor is it my focus. I'm working to bring a variable in what I believe religion itself eliminated. Because for me religion is the enemy and spirituality is the way to go. Faith partners with the spiritual, fear partners with the religious. Even the word *religion* itself means to return to bondage. That is NOT what I'm getting at. Faith is not linear. It is fluid; it changes, rearranges, reinvents, renews, and restores. It takes us to places we haven't been to in our minds, hearts, or even in our imaginations! That kind of creativity and dreaming are what have taken us from the day the Wright brothers created an airplane to the billion-dollar industry of artificial intelligence showing up in most big tech companies. The ability to go to a three-dimensional world via electronic goggles, and being able to be somewhere else in our mind when our body doesn't move at all, at one point had to be someone's dream. It is these kinds of dreams—being able to see someone via video on our phones, to connect to the Internet while we drive our cars with onboard routers, and even imagining taking a jet to Mars—that have moved us along in the business world.

And it all started because someone—usually someone who thinks differently than most people—wouldn't accept the limits of his or her current existence or surroundings.

The world is changed by anomalies. My faith path is not what I'm asking you to follow or even model. It's bigger than that. I believe that we were all given unique gifts, talents, abilities, and passions when we were knit inside of our mother's womb. We come into this life with those as driving points to all that we'll do. Depending on whether you were raised in a powerful or a controlling home, you might not even know what those things are. Look at it this way: deposited inside of you is a gift, talent, ability, and passion that I NEED for you to fulfill. We all do. We all need each other to fulfill our purpose and to fly as high and as hard as possible with all we've been given. This is when the anomalies will rise to their highest place and we'll start to see the change we need in our world. If they don't, and we continue to repeat history, we'll end up with more of what we already have and, sadly, be in more trouble than we already are now.

ANOMALY ACTION: THE MORNING RITUAL

So many of you feel called to start your own business and at the same time, to fulfill your purpose for your life. Ironically, my calling is to help you grow in your faith while growing a successful business—whatever that faith looks like to you—so you can support your family, live your dreams, and make a positive and lasting impact on the world. One of my greatest tools for creating success in business and in life is a simple but powerfully effective morning ritual. It was instrumental in helping me make my first million so I want to share it with you.

1. Begin your day by spending time alone and quiet the world around you.

Many people wake up and stumble into their days without intention or purpose. The way I'm wired won't let me do that. If I do, I'll never accomplish what's in front of me, let alone be present for it all. I have to have an intention or purpose or I'll sink. If I don't step into my greatest self every day then I'll just sink back and become what I don't want to be: the status quo. Sure, I feel the pull of e-mails and texts begging for my attention. It's so tempting, isn't it, to start the day on autopilot, moving from one task to another? But those things can wait. I feel called to start the day by focusing my mind and my spirit on what matters most—being a true and genuine steward and using my unique talents and gifts as I serve the world and love my customers. It is my belief that attending to the deepest needs of our soul will actually help make our businesses prosper more than we could ever dream was possible. Inviting heaven into everything I do has been the most life-changing thing I've ever done in business.

2. Ask heaven for guidance—and not just on personal matters.

Invite God and people to partner with you in your business. And when you ask questions, be prepared for answers. It might surprise you to know that this is one of the biggest reasons for my success. Even when I get answers in ways I don't expect—which happens all the time—I listen and act accordingly. Sometimes the answers scare me; sometimes they make no sense. But they are always significant. I understand who my business partner is, and I trust that completely. So, one of my most powerful business strategies is to simply ask God what I need for today. I ask Him for sustenance, wisdom, and inspiration to live my day in a way that is loving and powerful.

It is amazing what can happen when you sit still with Papa God and ask him questions. Maybe that's not going to be the answer you're searching for. So sit and be still in a space that does serve you well, with nature, a trusted friend, or maybe your journal.

3. Don't allow this incredible process to become scripted or mundane.

That doesn't work for those of us who don't follow a scripted path. Switch things up! I'm a very fluid and organic person, so if my morning routine starts feeling too routine, I'll change the scenery or some aspect of my practice. Sometimes I wake up with a mental block, and I feel like for some reason I can't pray. But I must pray. But who is to say that prayer must be uttered in words? On those days I dance! Or I might just lie on the floor and be quiet and let some music awaken my spirit. I fill my senses with beauty and joy, and heaven does the rest.

Promise me this—that you will start your day with a morning ritual. It could be the one I describe above or one of your own choosing. Make it your intention to invite help into your heart, into your day, and into your decisions—and not just in your personal life, but also in your business. I invite Papa God to partner with me, and this enables me to achieve supernatural results. You simply can't go wrong with giving a half hour every morning to something or Someone greater than yourself. Spend this sacred and quiet time with no agendas and no goals. Rest your restless mind. Be still. Receive new energy, as well as ideas and strategies for each new day. Embrace them!

Grab a Journal!

What's something you've always wished could be a part of your day that you tend to reserve only for "special days" when you get to do what you want? Write this out. Journal why you may have gotten to the place of allowing yourself to only have these things on special days. Could you begin to do these things daily or on days that your work output is really critical? What if it's a big thing, like climbing 10 miles up a mountain, but you change that to going for a walk outside, or in the mountains, for a half hour a few times per week. My point is this: How can you be good to yourself, with your morning ritual, and create an environment within for your best ideas to flow?

RESISTANCE: LET COURAGE BE YOUR SHIELD

The story you've always told yourself and the lies of the enemy will rise up strong when you invite change into your business. It will happen as you explore ways to quit a job that's stifling you, or to move away from a community in which your true self is suppressed, or to liberate yourself from a relationship that is holding you back. It will happen as you start your own business, and begin living your dreams and envisioning your success.

The bigger you dream and the more success you envision, the more resistance will show up. Think of it this way: your expansion into Papa God's dream for your life is an invitation for resistance to show up at your door. You may think it's uninvited, but it's not. Resistance is the enemy of growth. It will show up on time, every time. Resistance is the enemy through and through, and it's the biggest liar to ever walk the earth. It sucks. It hurts. It destroys!

Just as you start to make concrete plans, like taking an online business course, or openly share with family members that you're taking a big step in your life, resistance will grow. It wants to overwhelm you, and to stop you from becoming what you are meant to be. What Papa created you to be.

Be prepared. Be courageous. Remember WHO you are. Invite the spiritual into your business. There is no better protection. Live in your truth and in your faith. And whatever you do, don't let anything stop you. The world needs businesses built on integrity and faith. The world needs anomalies.

The world needs *you*.

> ### Spiritual Takeaway
> I am wise, powerful, and strong when I invite that which is greater than me to partner with me, not only in my life, but in my work as well. All of heaven is cheering me on.

CHAPTER 3

HIDDEN

Learning to hide started at a young age for me. The effects of trauma and abuse I endured as a child plagued me throughout most of my life. The story I believed about myself was this one: "I am broken. No one will love me. They can see my pain. My shame is dirty and I don't fit in. I must become someone I am not so that no one ever sees who I really am. Everyone will know if I try to break free, so it's easier to hide."

We all know it's not easier to hide. As a matter of fact, neuroscience teaches us that when we live in this duality—feeling our pain and shame and then hiding and covering it, we can create a breach in our DNA that will break down our health, our memory, and ultimately, cause inflammation and chronic pain. I was there, and I used my pain as the reason I had to hide, shelter myself, stay away from crowds, people, connection in general. Dr. John Sarno is a pioneer in the mind-body connection, in which emotional pain and rage trapped in the muscles causes physical pain. He states:

> The interaction between the generally reasonable, rational, ethical, moral, conscious mind and the repressed feelings of emotional pain, hurt, sadness, and anger characteristic of the unconscious mind appears to be the basis for mindbody disorders. *The Divided Mind* traces the history of psychosomatic medicine, including Freud's crucial role, and describes the psychology responsible for the broad range of psychosomatic

illness. The failure of medicine's practitioners to recognize and appropriately treat mindbody disorders has produced public health and economic problems of major proportions in the United States.

The Divided Mind: The Epidemic of Mindbody Disorders, 2007

I'd find many years later that my ability to hide and be alone to gain strength was a good thing woven into my DNA. When I no longer used it as a way to isolate myself, but rather to rejuvenate and renew myself, it became something that to this day gives me incredible power. The best way I can describe this would be to say I'm an introvert/extrovert. My need to be alone and renew and restore is just as great as my need to be with people, interact with them, and feed off their energy. Being both, it's important for me to make sure I have alone time when my public side of life is going to be needed, in things like public speaking or my social media content and coaching. I love helping people to remember who they are, find their innate gifts and talents, and turn those gifts into a profitable business or ministry! It's something I was born for; I love to do it, and we've had great results in my company when I am "on." But then I need to be alone in total silence. There's a great desire inside my soul to just be STILL. To not think, give, receive, or do anything at all. I must simply be alone in the silence. This is why you can find me running to the desert or the mountains to gain renewed strength or vision. I can be found lying by my pool in the sun, without anyone else there, just enjoying the incredible Arizona dry heat and listening to some soft music or the sounds of nature. The very same part of my soul that needs to be alone to renew, when coupled with pain and trauma, became isolated, reclusive, and very self-protective. As healing came in, my truest energetic self was released and my need to be alone transformed into new ways of renewal. Now when I tell others I need to be alone, they know it's a good thing, not a defensive act.

HOW PAIN TRANSFORMED INTO STRATEGY

Even as I type this, I am reminded of how hard I worked to keep walls around me. Abuse taught me suffering. Trauma taught me pain. But my own mind created a prison I couldn't get out of. Ironically, this was the single greatest reason why I didn't create a brick-and-mortar business, or do anything traditional at all in my career. The very thing that could have broken me for a lifetime, however, became the tool that Papa God would help me use to draw out my gifts, talents, and ultimately, my expertise as a businesswoman.

The Internet provided a protective covering, if you will, from real relationships, but it still enabled me to create what I thought was a persona, an identity that left me in control while I reached for my goals. Write this down: *control is a painful master.* It never has enough, never is satisfied. It's the wicked cousin of resistance, and while we serve control, we're brought into its web of intoxicating driven-ness that can cause us to never sleep, neglect our health, live a fake identity, and completely disconnect from reality. I believe this is what workaholism is, and it is a lie that teaches us we can work like a crazy person for five years, ignore everything else in life, and then lift our head up to find the great life we've created. When in reality, we'll look up in five years and find our relationships destroyed, our bodies exhausted, and a very weak foundation on which to build a business or anything else on. While I didn't go that far—completely disconnecting from reality—I did disconnect from others to the point that there were only a few people interacting with me on any close level at all for more than three quarters of my career.

Isn't it something that I could withdraw from people that much, while at the same time developing the skill of observation? Building a website and creating an e-mail to interact with my customers required an understanding of human behavior. So, while I was at home raising my children in my private, secluded existence, I also got really good at understanding and watching human behavior. In my mind I thought I was mastering the skill of marketing and copywriting. But when I heard an expert named Dan Kennedy say that copywriting was more of a science than anything—the science of watching human behavior—I had my first realization that maybe, just maybe, I had a gift that was very unique and could make me hugely wealthy.

I got really good at watching and identifying trends and patterns. Come to think of it, my whole life I've been constantly looking for trends, patterns, and pathways into something no one else is doing. Upon discovering the direct response marketing that we did in the early 2000s, I quickly understood that it didn't require that we meet people in person or even face to face. It was the great breakthrough of the Internet, and the great breakthrough for me in my career. I could build relationships and connections without ever really seeing people face to face, or really having a close relationship with them. Copywriting became my weapon of choice, and I got really, really good at it. Being able to persuade, influence, and direct people through stories and the written word opened up a whole new world for me. But at the same time, it reinforced and continued to teach me the mastery of hiding.

Trauma started the story, but *I* created a limiting belief that told me that other people were unsafe, so I hid behind my computer. I hid for over 12 years before I would come out to actually meet people in person. Never having to let anyone see into my soul or my life was the only way I could protect myself from the pain that I had known most of my life. Isn't it sad and funny at the same time, the stories we create for ourselves? The very thing I thought would protect me almost destroyed me.

Almost. But when I found safety in the comfort of my relationship with a very real, present, and living Papa God, my heart opened up and was healed so that I could let others into my life. Letting go of the control gave me more courage. Letting go of the things I thought I had to always keep and hold together gave me more strength.

He would meet me as I sank to the bathroom floor overwhelmed by motherhood and feeling like a complete failure. The cold floor oftentimes felt like the punishment I deserved for such horrific failure. Rather than being patient, I got irritated by my kids' energy. Noise intolerance. I had three sons and suffered from an anxiety that would shake me, startle me, and give me panic attacks every time my boys would squeal or scream. So I'd hide in the bathroom, crying into a towel so my babies couldn't hear me. "Why did you give me to them? They deserve better. I can't do this. There's no one who is helping me. I'm doing this all alone. I have so much pain inside of me, how the heck can I ever be a good mom?" Tears would run down my face, and I'd want to hide and run and scream all at the same time. The emotions were powerful, but my resolve to be a good mother was even more powerful. Those meetings on the bathroom floor with Papa were some of the shaping sessions of my future as a CEO and businesswoman. I experienced complete desperation to the point of wanting to die at times.

I wasn't really suicidal. I just felt like death would be the ultimate act of hiding, and I didn't want to come out back to my horrific life for a long time. My life felt like one long saga of failed attempts. The story I kept telling myself might be the very same story you tell yourself—that you're not good enough, smart enough, or strong enough to do what you've been designed for. As I began to explore the things that my soul craved and my heart ran after, it always seemed like there wasn't enough of me to fulfill the call of destiny.

If the pain didn't leave, the fear of getting stuck in it plagued me. Visions of my children never growing up, of me never getting off the tile floor in the bathroom, and of life passing by outside my 1,000-square-foot home haunted me. Good thing that's not how life works. Even when we're struggling and suffering and hiding in our torment and pain, life still goes on. This "still going on" I often felt in the spirit realm. The universe has been set into motion, it will continue forward whether we do or not. I wanted to hide, disappear, and vanish. Yet this pull for "still going on" was often swirling around me. This pull said that one day I would wake up to the story of my life, and that I could either begin to write it as I wanted or . . . it would continue to go on no matter what. I might just end up reading my own history played out without any input from me. If you're living there right now, feeling like life is going on and you can't seem to make it stop, rather than trying to stop it, what if you change yourself? What if we begin to invent the possibility together that you can change, things can change, and there's never an end to what we can all do? There's always possibility and always opportunity, for as long as the universe continues, we can get back up and move on in a new way through simple choices we make every day.

I imagined myself still on the floor of the bathroom while my sons went on without me, and I imagined them one day in college telling stories of how their crazy mother never came out of the bathroom again. I imagined TV show hosts telling the story of the little ole lady lying on the bathroom floor for 30 years. Connected to the Internet, no less, running a 2-million-dollar E-commerce business. Dear God. That got me off the floor.

Use this exercise to help you keep perspective in the challenging days of life and work:

7 days, 7 weeks, 7 months, 7 years—think forward.

- Where will you be 7 days, weeks, months, and years from now?
- Where could you be?
- Where do you want to be?
- When we make decisions, or maybe refuse to make decisions, staying passive and stuck, are we creating the kind of life we want to live and want to see?
- How will this matter 7 days from now?
- How will this play out 7 weeks from now?
- Will this matter as much 7 months from now?
- Ultimately, in 7 years, what could be the result or fruit of this time period in my life?

This is what moves me forward.

This is what causes me to get up when everything in my mind and body wants to just roll over and go back to sleep.

LIFE GOES ON

Thank God life still goes on.

This was the pattern and trend for me . . . I'd feel like crap, sink to the floor, hide in the towels crying, and life still went on, the boys were still outside the door waiting for me, my husband still came home every night, meals still needed to be cooked, laundry still had to be done . . . my ability to see all of this was most likely what kept me alive and from sinking into absolute disassociation from reality, and from disappearing from myself forever.

My inward life and outward existence were often in conflict. This disappearing from myself fantasy never did quite manifest. THANK GOD. But as the "still going on" world continued to spin forward, its daily demands quite literally pulled me out of hiding more times than I can even count.

Maybe you're there now.

Reading all of this makes you realize you're not alone, though you're struggling and suffering at your lowest point too. Maybe your bathroom floor is your car. You hide there. Maybe that's where you do your thinking, or your crying, or your plotting on how you'll disappear from yourself forever. And my story stirs something in you to believe there could be more. But how do you get past the obstacles, like I did?

Two big keys:

1. Don't allow yourself to get stuck.

2. Take it one day at a time.

Walking out of pain and into power doesn't happen because a psychiatrist writes us a prescription, or gives us a plan, and we wake up to a new day and a new life within 30 days. No matter how many times people promise us that we can change our lives that quickly, the real down and dirty no one wants to talk about—but all successful people have lived—is that we have to walk toward "walking out of pain." We have to step into our "stepping into power." Quite frankly, sometimes medication can help, or supplements, or hormones, or even all three. But the plan and the process will only work together when we make that decision to not get stuck and to continue forward one day at a time.

Keep the big picture in mind. Remember the seven-year focus. Make a decision that no matter what, you won't get stuck. You won't let the current reality that you're facing become your story. Realize that your current struggle won't end up being your destiny if you work to not get stuck.

Let me warn you, there will be days when the cold bathroom floor and screaming or crying into a towel will seem like a 5-star resort compared to the often terrifying new things we must try and believe in to create a new life, in both our personal and professional lives. But the hardest part isn't the stepping forward and the continuing on. No, the hardest part is knowing that we are capable of that, and yet we stay put. Knowing we need to walk away from that toxic relationship that is making us want to disappear from our own lives, yet doing nothing. That's the death of it all right there: to do nothing.

If you have people in your life who make you want to quit, it's time to love yourself and make a decision that you are more valuable than this and you are going to make a change. Put up better boundaries and define what they are. If necessary, end the relationship. But realize that to do nothing is always going to be harder, ultimately, than to move forward, even if you don't have all of the answers right now.

Maybe you have a situation at work that seems impossible. If the universe keeps going on and you will one day wake up seven years from now living your life—do you still want to live this, day in and day out, for seven more years? If your answer is no, and I pray it is, then start making those hard choices now. I bet you already know what most of these things are. The decisions that must be made many times are very clear. It's the walking out these choices daily that will change us.

This is what happened when I made a decision to fire the CEO that wasn't well suited for my company, despite the fact that we all liked him as a person. It's what caused me to reinvent my business strategies when I realized I didn't want to be like everyone else, even at the risk of being misunderstood. It's what gave me courage to end a 24-year marriage that I had worked very, *very* hard to make look perfect and everything I dreamed it could be (but knew in my heart of hearts, it was not). The pain of walking forward, of being judged, misunderstood, and a host of other questions plagued me for many years. But then I realized that a choice had to be made. A decision was going to be a critical component of writing my future, if I didn't want to wake up 70 years old still suffering, feeling unloved, abused, and neglected. Despite my fears, worries, insecurities, doubts, and so many pieces yet unknown, I chose life for myself. I chose a different story, a different future, and I filed for that divorce. It was one of the hardest things I've ever walked out on, because I came face to face with all the unhealed places in my life. A bright light from heaven revealed all the areas of my heart that were darkened, numb, and dying. Trust me, I didn't expect or want this when I made my decision and began to walk it out. Now, I wanted a fairy tale story of a new life that was waiting for me, with a new man, a new existence, and my happily ever after story to appear. But life doesn't work that way.

Maybe you're there too, and you have to make some decisions. It might be the hardest thing you've ever done in your life: choosing to let go of the pain of someone who betrayed you, and making a choice to learn to love and trust again. It could be something in your work life or in your personal life. I believe they will always intersect and cross over anyway, so who really cares what "life" it is. There's a gaping hole, a heavy weight, a long-carried burden that must be laid down for you to be able to do all that you're called to and for you to receive all that you desire and deserve. Make that choice. Walk out that decision. Never back down from pursuing the best that life has for you.

As I look back, it's become quite apparent that for me this pull of "still going on . . . will you join us and go on too?" was actually Papa God and all the angels breathing life over me when I felt nothing but death.

I'm breathing life over you right now, too, and asking you to take that first step toward freedom.

Take one day at a time. It would have been easy to drown in the process of change I had to go through. Some days felt like it was so difficult I just wanted to stay in bed all day, or run to the mountains and never come back. Journaling helped me and still helps me to make my way through all of the feelings, struggles, and fears. Many times you will probably feel like you can't sort through all of the new things that come up. Healing, growing, and moving into all that we are is like that. I want to reassure you that in the process you might not be able to sort through it all, but one day you'll look back and read your journal entries and see the great unfolding that was occurring. So take good notes. Pour it out. Process those feelings and fears on paper. You'll have so much to share with all of us as you continue on.

You could be a business owner like me, or a mom who feels completely inadequate just as I have. Or maybe you're both, and can really relate to my experience of feeling really powerful in some spaces in my life and without any power in others. Either way, this one thing I know to be true: the place where we want to hide and disappear the most is most often the place where Papa God will show up, turn the lights on, and make something incredible out of our shame.

Hiding and shame are synonymous. Being vulnerable enough to admit we want to hide because we feel this horrific, dark, "I don't fit in anywhere" shame will open doors we never thought could exist.

THE PERFORMER

Hiding can show up in all kinds of extreme ways. It can even masquerade as being successful when in reality it's covered up with so many layers, we've lost ourselves deep within our own skin.

I remember a day in my life when I felt that way. I was in my 20s and chasing after a dream, but got caught in the spiral of performance. My body hurt. My mind was weak. My body fat was below 4 percent. As I stood backstage at the Mount Pleasant Bodybuilding Championship, what should have felt like a dream come true felt like a sick joke of an existence. No carbs had entered my body for more than 10 days, and the lack of water had created skin that looked like it had been Saran-wrapped over my muscles and tendons. Overcoming every voice of resistance, submitting to every rule required, the mental games and tricks I fought while forcing my body beyond its own emotions and feelings created inside my soul a warrior-like commitment to deny myself, and make my own existence obey a goal. That day I went beyond all of my expectations. Nevertheless, my body hurt, my brain felt beyond numb, and my tongue was so dry I choked to even swallow as I walked on stage.

There she was, the performer. She could smile and flex, even in pain. She grabbed the audience's attention in just seconds, as her biceps and quads busted through her paper-thin skin. Her tan, lean, and shredded body became her trophy, and she would earn a huge one at the end of the day. But the hiding continued. Behind the smile, the sex appeal, the disciplined warrior-focus, was still me—a young girl trying to disappear from her own life. Ribbons were placed around my neck for best arms, most ripped abs, and the biggest back they had ever seen on a woman of my petite size. Cheers and honor were given beyond anything expected, and all I felt was a growing need to run, hide, and sleep. Sleep for a long, long, long time, hoping to wake up to a better life one day, a life in which I didn't feel the need to hide anymore. I refer to myself as "she" here because that's what being someone other than who we really we are can feel like. As if we're watching a movie of someone else—all the while it's us, attempting to live our life but denying who we really are.

To say I was depressed is an understatement. I quit that night. Quit the sport, quit the commitment, quit the diet, the culture, the physical shock, and the torture. All I wanted to be was who Papa had made me to be. To live beyond the expectations of others, the fear of failure, the horrific discipline that got me to a mindless state. Deep within me there was a crying out for truth, for more, and for love.

Isn't it something that we can live through such intense suffering and wake up one day to see that the life we were dreaming about is now our existence? The pain is gone, the shame was removed, the wanting to disappear has been replaced with being found and free, and we can see with 20/20 vision what the root was.

BIG-PICTURE LESSON

My hiding and hidden state always led me to a point of desperation that was fuel that led me to fight for more.

Maybe you're there now too. This fight led me to who you see today. I'm not a perfect woman, nor do I ever want to be. But I know who I am. I know without a shadow of a doubt that I am loved. It's nonnegotiable in my life now. The deep, deep love of Papa has quieted and filled all the empty corridors of shame that lived inside of me all those years. Do I still struggle with insecurity, fear, and a sense of wanting to run? Yes. Nearly every new deep relationship that is brought into my life brings with it the quick desire to want to disappear within. But now I'll talk about it, let people know what I've been through, and how much I want to stay free. And I'll let them love me, help me, and hold me up when I can't hold myself up on my own.

I've walked through a lot of healing, counseling, forgiving, and releasing to even be able to share any of this with you. If it helps just one person to open the door to their hidden life, it will be worth it all. We can all live extraordinary and fulfilling lives. I am proof, and you can be too.

Many of us withhold our divinely given gifts from the world because we don't feel whole or we're hiding in shame. Maybe you too have been wanting to disappear from your own life while the rest of the world is "still going on." This leads us to hiding our talents, keeping our gifts dormant, and never reaching our full destiny, as Papa God designed. We might live in a false identity, seeking to protect and hide the pain.

But our hearts cry out for more. Even when we're lying on the bathroom floor, hiding in the car, and pretending in the middle of our performances that we're okay when we know we're not, there's a small burning fire inside each of us that cries out to be free.

The question becomes, "What will we do with our gifts?"

What can we tangibly and practically do to learn to live just one level higher than where we are now? It has to be practical or, face it, we'll never follow through. Living in the freedom that Papa gave requires a daily walking it out and a "still going to go on, no matter what" attitude. So how can we do this now, today?

In the following pages are a few things I've learned along the way in my own journey that ultimately led to life and freedom. I might add, life and freedom I was *destined* for. Yes, it has been amazing this transformation I'm living, in so many wonderful ways. The triumphs that I have experienced have many times been such mountaintop experiences! But when all is said and done, I can tell you with all my heart, the real wars, the real blood, guts, and tears battles were fought while lying on a floor, sobbing my eyes out to Papa and begging Him to make me free.

The floors have changed. I'm no longer in the bathroom, crying and hiding. Now I'm in my office, letting Papa use me to impact other people's lives, and my day oftentimes starts out in tears on the floor, sucking carpet, and crying my eyes out, begging Him to make me a better woman. My desire to be free has never stopped, and I pray it never does for you as well.

ANOMALY ACTION: MY CORE BELIEFS

Look where all my cries for help led me and where I ended up! What an honor it is today to be able to share with you powerful action steps that you can use now. Below are some of my own core beliefs that have helped me to be successful. May they inspire you to come up with a few nonnegotiable core beliefs for your own life. These tips shaped my life and are empowering my future every single day. They might do the same for you!

Never live your life alone.

We are created for community and for each other. We were not designed to be alone. If you are surrounded by negative people who don't believe in your dreams, you may feel terribly isolated or unseen. I'm here to tell you that there is no reason for you to have to suffer like that. Reach out, and please, find good people to connect with. Toxic friends and family can destroy dreams, and you are worth so much more. Don't wait for your group of people that you feel at home with to find you. Go find them, NOW!

Look online for groups in your local community. Push aside the struggle to just stay put; do one thing every day that is uncomfortable and unfamiliar. Be willing to relocate, redesign your life, and to start anew. Who cares what your family has always done, or what you've always known? You will no longer seek to disappear. It's time for your best self to rise up!

Never give up on your dreams.

Whether you believe in Papa God or not, I'm here to tell you that you were *not* created to live a meager existence of going from one act of survival to the next. This constant pull to disappear must be met with the reality that life is "still going on" and we have to get up now and do something. We have been designed to dream. God WANTS us to live a life that is beyond ourselves. He designed us that way.

The first time I heard the saying "It's not about you," I thought it was the biggest lie ever. Of course it's about me! I need to be free—my dreams are dying inside me, and I have a constant desire to run away and disappear! I'd later realize that these feelings are also felt by millions of other people every single day, and that Papa wanted to use my pain to help me find His—and my own—true purpose. There were others that I was fighting for every time I turned around, came back, stopped running, and faced my fear. Many of these "others'" are you, my readers. You were the ones I was fighting for as I woke up to my truth and spoke up with my power. You could be pioneering a path for others too. You could be breaking ground for those who need a new place to walk. Fight your war! We need you to!

There are people out there who really need YOUR dreams to happen. They need your unique brilliance, perspective, experience, and wisdom. While you're thinking that you're just fighting to break free in your own life, you're actually making a difference in the spirit realm, and in history, for generations to come. There are future generations of people who need you to take flight on the things that Papa God gave you. Never ever give up on your beautiful dreams, no matter how wild and crazy they may seem. Write them down, visualize them, strengthen your gifts, and move forward in what has been given to you.

Work with someone who has what you desire and what you are gifted to do.

Whether it's a mentor in business, music, marketing, or even writing, work with someone who has the unique talents and abilities to help you realize your dreams. This is why I mentor thousands of small business owners and fight for their freedom every single day. I want to pass the baton, be a source of encouragement, and make a difference. I didn't just fight for my own life; the lessons I learned ended up being what I can now impart to them. I pulled down from heaven not only what I needed, but what they will need too.

Find someone with whom you can connect spiritually, emotionally, and in business, someone who holds a truth that resonates with you. Don't settle on this one, or that one, or compromise simply because someone looks super successful. What we compromise on, we'll lose. Don't trade in the vision that Papa God gave you for marketing strategies that are aligned with things you can't partner with. Stay true to you. Seek out a mentor who speaks truth, speaks your potential, and one who will love you through every single phase of the journey. Yes, I said love. Find a leader who leads with love and can help you fulfill your purpose and destiny!

Here are a few practical tips in finding a mentor or coach who is perfectly aligned with you:

- Is your potential mentor's worldview similar to yours? If you are a spiritual person it's probably not a good idea to have a long-term mentor who is not. While I've worked and learned from people who believe differently than I do, if they were set to change me rather than giving me some wisdom and knowledge I was lacking, it became apparent that we couldn't work together for a long time.

- Does your potential mentor have past experience that you can learn from and relate to? What is their track record? Don't focus on just one great accomplishment. Does their track record hold the knowledge you lack, so that you can move forward in all that you're called to do?

- Does your potential mentor have current knowledge of what you need? Old-school wisdom of marketing is going to come up short in the world of social media. The knowledge of nutrition from the 70s would be pretty outdated compared to today's research.

- Who are they as a person? It's important to find out as much as you are able to about what kind of person your mentor is. Can you find things they support and talk about and that inspire you? What about accomplishments and values? Did they build a business, or become the best singing coach in the world but neglected their family? Look for these things. Ask a lot of questions.

- Check out their social media profiles. Do you see a growing person or what appears to just be a marketing persona? See how other clients and followers interact with their pages and how they talk back. If they talk back! This can show us the humanity and many times be the thing that either really connects us to them or helps us to see that we're not a good match.

WELCOMING NEW LIFE

When you think that the wild and ridiculous couldn't happen, it's time for you to pack your bags—because you're on your way! Things can change in ways that we never expect—and faster than we had planned.

Just when I thought my life was over and the last saga of my drama was about to unfold, Papa God blew a new life right into me. He knocked the negative draining wind out of me and gave me a fresh vision and hope for my future.

You just never know when your breakthrough will happen. Many times, all of the things that didn't break you are proof that your breakthrough is on its way! These trials and struggles will be waved as banners of celebration that you didn't give up. Just as you're reading my words right now because I never quit, you too will be leading someone in your future, and they'll celebrate your persistence with you as well!

All of heaven reached down and took a woman who knew shattering pain and enormous success and gave her the desire to go further. I am here to tell you that right when you think the wild and ridiculous can't happen, you'd better start packing for the journey ahead! I believe faith can take us further than anything in life. Hustle and a résumé can't take you as far as favor and faith will! Yes, you're going to have to work hard, and yes, you'll need experience and skill, but it might shock you how Papa God can even use your pain to help you master your purpose! It still shocks me every single day that I get to live such a life as mine. But really, it shouldn't shock me. I was BORN FOR THIS. And so were you!

Faith in the impossible, faith that will believe when no one else will. Against every odd, obstacle, and experience you've had thus far, your future life and business can be rewritten and restored, and nothing is too big to hold you back when you simply BELIEVE.

It's not very common to hear about faith in business or at work. Some people think that faith doesn't belong at all in work. I say it belongs at work, was made for the business realm, and it's time to open the windows on the possibility. It takes faith to follow your dream, faith to press past all of the fear and doubt, and faith to allow Papa God to use you, even when you're healing, even when you're imperfect and desperately in need of His help!

Grab a Journal!

Did sharing my key core beliefs trigger identifying your own for you? All this talk of being our best selves, becoming more, resisting the temptation to strive, press, and perform can bring up some stuff. Write that stuff down now. Don't look for answers just yet; let the pages of your journal just become a safe place where you can "dump" it all. It is in these brain dumps that we can find our truest selves and the loudest voice of resistance we're fighting. Write it down now.

RESISTANCE: NOWHERE TO HIDE

Resistance never sleeps. It will fight you in your sleep and torment you again the second you wake up. If you've fought the war of resistance long enough and hard enough only to fall flat on your face in self-doubt and fear every single time, you'll begin to hide.

Resistance will try to silence you like it silenced me even as a child. And there's something deep inside of me that doesn't like to be shut up or silenced. But I didn't realize it until I was a mother of three grown sons. Until then, my habit became to hide. Hide from close relationships with people and hide from the pain and trauma so that no one ever knows the things I've lived through. Hide my dreams, my visions, my passions, the fact that I see angels, and can see colors around people. Hide it all.

Resistance will disguise itself as fear, self-doubt, and even panic, and it will try to fill you with reasons to hide. To stop growing. To stop believing in yourself. To stop moving forward. But hear this from someone who knows: You can overcome resistance. You truly can. You can step out of hiding and into the light of Papa God's love. Do what I have done—and what has never failed me. Invite Papa God into every aspect of your life. Let Him bring light into the hidden corners of your brokenness. Align your beautiful dreams with His purpose for your life. Choose faith over fear. Every time. And when you are living your dreams, as I am living mine, pay it forward. Share your message with someone who needs to hear it. Weaken the power of resistance for yourself and for those who follow.

Why would we ever expect people to satisfy us when Papa God has given us *everything*?

> ## Spiritual Takeaway
> I have faith in the future despite what the past says and what the present might be saying even in this moment. I will never lose my faith, no matter what happens. The world needs me to fulfill my destiny. I will push the hiding and disappearing aside, and step out into the light I was made for!

CHAPTER 4

THE MOTHER OF ALL POSSIBILITIES

Sometimes we're living our life and think "this is it." We'll get the kids ready for school in the morning while we get ready for work, and the same day-in, day-out activities can zap us of courage, strength, and even the ability to fight back with faith. If we can get a bigger picture of what's possible even in our mundane, everyday things, we'll see that we were never meant to just survive or "just get by." The battle of trying to not fit in—and to be who we were created to be—will require a bigger vision, a heart open to possibility and a down-and-dirty drive to *never* quit.

As a young mother I learned that I had two choices: see the problem or see the possibility beyond it. Maybe you've been raised by a parent who sees all of the problems and the negative side of things. It can damage you deeply. My own childhood was not filled with hope and excitement, but rather, pain and the pressure to perform and always be perfect. I didn't want that for my children. I knew I could become what I knew growing up, or reinvent a future for my children that would follow them into adulthood.

Possibility was the antidepressant that I needed in my life. Seeing the possibility in things that were challenging, falling apart, or beyond my control prepared me for business. It was just what my children needed, as well. Life as a young mom can get very challenging. I remember difficult days that I swore would not end and seasons when it felt like nothing would change and I'd be in a struggle with diapers, the flu, and discouragement FOREVER. But possibility taught me to see more, and to see beyond where we were. It kept me from sinking. Even now, as I run my company, interact with millions of people on social media, battle some health challenges that require ongoing treatment, and experience the ups and downs of life as a business owner, possibility is still a powerful thread in my life and my business.

You see to me, possibility is rooted in faith. Having faith to be your anomaly, out-of-the-box, different self will move you forward. There's no one who will ever be able to move you forward like the deep call within that knows it was never created to conform. Think about it. When faced with a challenge, no matter how big or small, we can feel defeated or we can find encouragement in seeing ourselves overcoming the challenge. This would happen when I was raising my three boys. I remember how many times they would lose things, for example. It's normal. They play and explore and build and create, and in their day-to-day lives, toys, shoes, homework—you name it—get misplaced.

Whenever my boys would come to me and ask me to help them find something they'd lost, they always asked me to pray. It was normal for me to pray about everything in our home. So they'd ask me to find their lost pencil, book, building block, truck, etcetera. Knowing I didn't want them to just hang on to Momma's faith, but that I wanted them to experience Papa God on their own as well, I would teach them how to "find lost things" by asking Him to intervene. It was a big faith builder for my little guys! "Ask Holy Spirit where it is, then go there." They would get so excited because every time, 100 percent of the time, Holy Spirit would place a picture in their small, powerful brains. They'd run to where the picture was and encounter the God that is there. To this day, my grown sons will text or call me because they can't find something that is really important for work, their involvement at church, or just as they're heading out the door for a day of fun. They will ask me to pray for them—because they're still asking me to pray about things that matter to them—and I'm still the first one to say, "Have you asked Holy Spirit where it is?" Even now, they're encountering God when they've lost drumsticks, headphones, or my grandson's favorite toy. Just this small lesson on faith has shaped my children. But you know it could have gone a completely different way.

Imagine if every time my explorers lost something, the first thing they heard from me were words of discouragement or judgment. "Seriously? You lost them AGAIN?! You're so absent-minded and can't keep track of anything!" Have you had such words of death spoken over you? Cancel it now. For me, I use a simple prayer like this: *I break that judgment off of me in Jesus's name!* Blame can be affecting everything you do today if you have woven deep inside your DNA the idea that you are absent-minded and can't keep track of a thing. I'm so grateful this is not the path I took in my mothering, and Papa used my time as a young mommy to teach me even more than I was teaching my kiddos.

Thinking back to my years as a young mother, there were so many times when possibility gave us courage to ask for the impossible and believe we could achieve even more. My youngest son has the gift of healing. I was able to see this at a very young age. Bobby knew that we all believed in miracles and more importantly, the God of miracles. It wasn't enough for me to teach them to just ask for a miracle—I wanted my children to know the One who wanted miracles to be the "normal" course of our life and not the exception. One day when he was about five years old, he came knocking on the garage door and asked me to come help him. As I came into the garage, I saw my full-of-faith, little-giant son carrying a dead bird. He looked at me with enough faith to move a mountain and said, "Momma, can we pray and raise this birdie from the dead?" My first thought was, *OMG we can do this!* My second thought was, *OMG the gerrrrmmmms!* His faith was so strong he believed that we could raise this little creature back to life. Sadly the little birdie was dead. He wasn't coming back to life. But Bobby believed so strongly that he could raise this little creature that he came to me, someone bigger than himself, to ask for help. Possibility was deeply woven into his DNA. Today he lives in a culture of belief and sees God move in miraculous ways. That was one fruit of me making a decision to see more, when I could have just sunk into negativity like so many others around me. It also was heaven's gift to me—sending me a son who had faith when I needed it!

THE IMPORTANCE OF FAITH

To be honest I really don't like a life devoid of faith. It hurts too much, makes my body sick, and causes me to hide in desperation. I don't do relationships with people who are negative, full of doubt, and always expecting the worst in situations. Sure, I'll love them and do what I can to influence them, but a deep friendship isn't going to happen. I'm wired with a gift of faith and a desire to believe for *anything*. God is so open to anything we can ask Him for or believe with Him on. It saddens me to see so many people in this world, in my business, and in my local church who are so full of doubt and fear. Living in fear and doubt is suffocating. There's no hope, room for growth, or chance to get better. That's just not for me! I'm sorry, but it feels like a slow death I don't want to experience.

Personally, I love to read all kinds of books about the giants in faith, those who moved mountains, transformed nations, fed babies, healed the sick, opened deaf ears, restored sight to the blind. I can*not* comprehend why the local church and most people I meet have no faith, or at best, are just barely hanging on. When people question my intention of always seeing the cup half full, wanting to see the possibility in pain and problems, and believing Papa cares about everything that matters to us, it makes me want to hide again. This broke me and made me run away from any form of community in my life. It was another key factor as to why I hid for so long from regular relationships and people in general. But Papa intervened. He would use my business to restore my need for love, and for people. He used my business as a place to heal me, restore me, and to help others learn to love too.

A VISION FOR YOUR LIFE

My early years as a momma taught me to ask Papa God for anything. My later years as a CEO taught me to believe in Papa God for everything. Our faith needs to grow from just waving SOS signals up to heaven, hoping someone or something hears us, to being a living, breathing, vibrant connection between us here on earth and all that is in heaven. It is my belief that all of heaven is cheering us on, and all we have to do is get into agreement with heaven to see worlds unknown right here on earth, in our day-to-day lives, and yes—in our businesses as well.

It's not my desire to just teach you how to believe bigger, and to go beyond your current life into something you survive. I see more for you. Imagine, if you will, the hardest seasons of your life becoming building blocks for everything you've ever wanted. The years of praying for Papa God to stretch your $5 so that you could get through the week on a quarter of a tank of gas; the times when you had no clue how to clothe your children, and then you found all that you needed given to you from an unsuspecting friend; and the times you battled health challenges and found healing. Being a person who lives a life that is bigger than you could have dreamed of takes more than faith. It takes vision.

Get a bigger picture of what could happen and allow yourself to see beyond just where you are now, in survival. Vision will hold you together like superglue when life throws trial after trial and pressure upon pressure on your dreams and belief. Vision will hold your focus and give you unstoppable resolve, when everything around you is falling apart. My life has not been easy; it never has. But I had a vision for who I could be and all that we could have, and was never ever willing to let it go. Vision will be a compass when you feel like the earth is shaking beneath your feet and you've lost your way. Vision will hold you when nothing else will.

Learning not to get stuck in your situation, circumstance, and pain will be key. Things can seem so thick it's like you can't breathe. There are going to be times in life when you'll feel as though you can't go on another minute, but you will. Learning to not get stuck in our current reality and keeping a vision of our goals, potential, and possibilities can change things quickly. It's a principle I first learned as a young mom who wanted to give up more times than I even care to remember, and later would be used a *lot* in my companies and business building. It helps me to not get sucked into and stuck in whatever reality I might be struggling with at the time, whether I'm learning how to better use our ad budget, deciding to let the wrong people who aren't a good fit for our business go, or plowing forward into new markets when I feel like just staying put. It's especially important when I feel like hiding to remind myself that refusing to get stuck is the focus, not being able to see how things will turn out. Shift your focus when you feel as though you're going to drown. Go watch a good cat video on YouTube! But seriously, find things that help you to shift quickly and use them as tools for focus. For me it's music, nature, and being in the sunshine. I reset quickly with the right music. I can refocus quickly with an hour break outside in the sun. Many times we want to see the end from the beginning to reassure ourselves that we'll make it. But that's not reality. Most times we can't see even the middle, let alone the end, and we have to have something beyond just faith to get us there. Vision and a strong commitment to not getting stuck will be powerful tools for taking you beyond just a survival mind-set. The very thing that you think will break you can be what ultimately saves you.

As a young mother who was also building a company, I would often feel like I was drowning. My "stick to it" attitude, my constant shift to the way I wanted to do things, and my anomaly, out-of-the-box way saved me from quitting many times. In later years, I'd discover it would become a tool that kept me going in many other aspects of life. This same kind of stick-to-it focus helped me relocate when internally I was facing a lot of fears. It helped me create a path to wean myself off of all opiates that I had been taking for my autoimmune conditions, when the "only way" the doctors gave me for such higher doses of medication would include massive withdrawal and suffering OR taking another drug to pacify my body out of its dependence.

I remembered so many times how I went through deep waters as a young mommy, and in my companies, and never died, and it gave me courage to create my *own path* off of this medication! Now I'm in the middle of creating a course that can help others do the same. I didn't become a statistic. My anomaly way of living once again served me well, and the possibility-in-pressure mind-set I learned as a mother saved me!

The goal is to keep moving in all your growth. Live in possibility and figure out what works for you in your day-to-day life. Just because someone else finds peace in planning everything out doesn't mean that will work for you! Maybe you're a clipboard and wing-it type person. Then wing it and wing it well! If you're the kind of person who is lost without a map, then create a daily living map that serves you well and live your life in confidence. Possibility can help you just let go of everyone's expectations and trainings that never helped and will empower you to just *do* what does work! For me, all of this inspiration and ability to keep going revolves around my belief in knowing that all of heaven is with me and that I'm never alone.

TRUE PRODUCTIVITY

Mothering and dependence on Papa taught me a whole new dimension of living that changed who I was and who my children and grandchildren would become. Sadly, the experience I was having didn't match the theology of most people I met. They thought I was "out there" and would oftentimes tell me to "buckle my seatbelt to stay planted here on earth." To them I was not relatable. I didn't fit in. This would lead me to more fear, isolation, hiding, and desperation, until Papa God began to do work I never expected. He began to teach me things that later in my career people would pay to learn from me.

Time and energy management is one of those valuable lessons. To say I was obsessed with productivity is an understatement. I was beyond obsessed. I wanted to master being productive, and powerful, and to get all that I could out of every hour that I worked on my businesses, and lived my daily life.

But as often happens to supercharged, adrenaline-running entrepreneurs, I would crash. Studying the numerous ways to manage my time, get more out of my day, survive with less sleep, get the slight edge with supplements, mind control, and any other trick I could find, my drive was overrun by my capacity. I burned out. This is when Papa began to teach me the difference between energy out and energy in, and how very, very different this was from just controlling every 15 minutes on my calendar. I began to see patterns and trends in my energy output, times when my bandwidth, so to speak, was higher and stronger during the day than at other times. I started to see when I was focused, clear, and powerful, and when I felt like I was just sleepwalking through my day. This newfound knowledge of energy vs. time would completely change how I ran my companies, lived my day-to-day life, and ultimately, how I'd plan for my future.

Energy is something we can feed, master, grow, and influence. Time is static. Just finding how much we can fit into each hour never worked for me because I'd want to stuff so much into one day no one could live it out. But I noticed that there was a pattern in my life when things worked really well—it was when I did the most demanding, creative, and "genius" type work early, early in the day. Sometimes as early as 3 A.M. This entire book was written before most people even wake up, because that's when I am LIT UP the most, and channeling that energy to serve me helped me to write without a ton of distractions. If I had written this book like others have taught, I would have had to carve out an hour a day for months. Blah. That never worked for me in any area of my life. Identifying WHEN I am the most energetic, focused, and clear and making a commitment to work within that time period caused me to multiply my productivity. Taking breaks, lying in the sun, and going to the gym when I was out of energy helped me to refuel throughout the rest of my day.

It wasn't so much about getting everything I could out of every day anymore; rather, it was about being my *absolute best* in anything that I did. Even if my best work happened only two hours on any given day, if that two hours was fully and powerfully executed, rather than just hours of unfocused distraction and weariness, I could accomplish more in those two hours than most people would be able to do in two days.

Understanding and being willing to admit that my best times in any given day are between 4:00 A.M. and 11:00 A.M., I could plan my most critical activities during these hours. This didn't mean I wouldn't work the rest of the day, but it did mean that when I had activities where my spirit, brain, and body needed to be at their best, I would make sure I did those things early on in the day.

Energy seems to beget more energy. Weariness and lack of focus tends to birth the same. So when we want more energy, we have to not only guard against weariness and lack of focus, we also have to pay attention to what causes us to go into these states.

HOW ENTREPRENEURS NEED TO USE ENERGY

Growing a business requires a lot of time and effort. But those things are not the same. Many new entrepreneurs—and even established business owners—make this same crucial mistake. They think hours equal effort. But rather than just marking off all your tasks and to-dos on a calendar by filling in each hour of the day and week, it's time we start paying attention to what tends to drain us—and how to cut it off at the source. Wrong relationships, lots of personal texting and e-mail interruptions during the day, drifting on social media or shopping sites when we should be focusing can destroy our efforts . . . it's time we start taking the steps we need to eliminate our drainers! This is the secret to how we'll get more done in less time and make more money with less stress. For example, if you know that meetings with your team or clients tend to go very well early on in the day, then stop coaching and consulting late at night or even in the afternoon. Go do a workout in the afternoon and do most of your business-related work before noon. Trust me, no one is ever going to show up and file a complaint against you as you begin to reinvent how you do life. It might feel like you're being watched, or judged, or even misunderstood, but oftentimes that's just mirroring neurons in our brain questioning what we've always known and always done, as we forge ahead along new pathways. Keep doing the things that serve you best without apology and you'll create new memories and new neurons that will reinforce your new beliefs and habits. This is why NO ONE can talk me into doing a speaking engagement late in the afternoon, nor can they pay me enough to jam into my day 20 hours of stress just for a bigger bottom line. I know myself and what supports me. I also know what tears me down, and I'm just not willing to go there anymore.

Decide to be *production focused*, rather than *time focused*. This will change your entire perspective. If you got done what was most important to you in only two hours, who says you're more powerful if you strive to stuff eight more hours of crap into your day to feel "legitimate"? You got done what was crucial! Go to the gym early. Take a hike, go shopping, take a nap, or go out to lunch with a friend. You earned the rest of the day to be what you want it to be, because the things you're committed to got done. Who cares how long it took you?

Look at what you have gotten done rather than all of the things that are still undone. This was critical for me as a young mother and is a governing factor in my life as a business owner. Have a "Got Done" list that is more important than your never-ending "To Do" list. Reward yourself for the small things and you'll be amazed by how much you actually are accomplishing every day. Don't get stuck in the overload of all the details. Even if you're a "detail to big picture" person, you can find a big picture inside many of the details that are connecting your path forward. Otherwise, if you are constantly walking around with an attitude of things "never getting done," you'll never get to where you are designed to be, and will most likely end up disillusioned and depressed.

BIG-PICTURE LESSON

Life as a mother, a business owner, and a homeschooler meant that things were never "all done." There was always something else that had to be attended to and completed. Yes, I homeschooled all three of my sons from K–12. As I look back on that today, I think to myself, *Were you insane?!* Yup, quite the overachiever. But that time period produced some of my most favorite memories of learning how to live like an anomaly, how to reinvent how things were done, and how to use my energy, and not just my time, to plant deep roots that serve my sons very well even today in their careers. Creating results didn't look the same every day. But the demands of every season helped me to learn, and to grow personally more than anything else in my entire life. I often say that while I've built more than 15 companies in my career, all of which have been successful, this is *not* my greatest work or the thing I am most proud of. Raising my sons— even while battling my own pain and horrific illnesses, feeling unloved in my marriage, and facing the remnants of childhood abuse that wanted to destroy my entire life—was my greatest accomplishment. Growing up with them, living life with them every single day, trusting Papa God with them, was the greatest thing I have ever done with and in my life. Knowing that helps me stay strong even when—especially when—things get tough.

ANOMALY ACTION: STRENGTH KEYS

We all have difficult seasons in life. One of the keys to staying strong in the face of your difficulties is to love yourself. To embrace that mind-set and to stay strong and persevere through challenging times personally or professionally, adopt these anomaly mind-set habits. Give yourself grace.

This is a time to embrace self-care and to support yourself. Take a little more time to get ready in the morning. Schedule in naps on the weekends. If you have a traditional job, there may even be times when you may truly need to take a few personal days. You cannot work if you are completely burned out. Don't beat yourself up or become your own worst enemy. You deserve grace, and grace will teach you how to say NO so you can say YES to your future.

1. Reach higher. I believe that spirituality is a source of comfort, strength, and wisdom for people who are going through depression or difficult challenges. I am an outspoken Christian and I love Jesus. But I also honor those who have different faiths. Regardless of your religious beliefs, when you are at your lowest, don't go it alone. Reach higher. I personally reach up to heaven for strength I don't have on my own. It helps me focus, renews my sense of courage, and gives me strength to endure. For you, it might mean that you reach out to friends, and go beyond yourself and your current situation. Just like when we talked about never going it alone in the last chapter, remember to reach higher with those you're doing life with. Hold each other up!

2. Keep moving. Your body, heart, and mind may be telling you to go into hiding to avoid any more possible stress. But this is not the time to get stuck. So keep moving. When you are feeling like you can't keep going, see if you can scale back your commitments but still stay in the game. Keep showing up in your life by going to work, keep showing up at the gym, and do your very best to keep your current commitments. What I don't want is for you to give up when it gets difficult. Because it will get difficult. Remember to keep an *energy* focus vs. a time focus. Many days you might feel like you're only operating at 25 percent of your normal capacity, but that 25 percent is a strong commitment and sure does beat quitting. Others might have quit, but you made a firm resolve to keep going. All of this adds up! When it comes to physical activity, your stress levels will be lower if you keep moving. Activity produces energy. Know when to rest and get good sleep, yes. But at the end of the day, even when you don't feel like doing it, overcome your feelings with a commitment to go the long haul. You'll be proud of your accomplishments once you reach the other side of this season. Make it your personal goal to stay in the game even though you might feel like you're not the best participant. Just the fact that you didn't quit will be something to celebrate when you cross the finish line.

I hope that these tips help you through any difficult season in life. I've been through health challenges, relationship struggles, and business successes and failures—all required that I keep a clear focus, give myself grace, reach higher, and stay in the game. Not every trial is created equal. These two tips might be all that you can do. That's okay. Just remember, we're all unique and we all handle stress and strain differently. Be good to yourself.

Grab a Journal!

Where do you need to reach higher? Do you need to set boundaries or tighten up the ones you have? Where do you need to give yourself grace to breathe, and where is it going to be critical to push yourself along? Write it all out. No rules, no filter. This is for your eyes (and soul!) only.

RESISTANCE: CREATING BOUNDARIES

As you reinvent and create possibility for yourself, your family, and your business, once again, resistance to the new you will show up. This time, not only will you be ready, you'll have a simple yet powerful tool that will help you fight back: the creation of boundaries. Block out family time in your schedule, and even if a client or customer is going to call with a multimillion-dollar deal, don't answer the phone. Be true to what matters to you and life will reward you with things beyond what you can even see. I know. It's the opposite of the advice you've heard about working hard, dedicating yourself to your career or new business, and never stopping until you've achieved success. But true success doesn't come that way. Burnout does. And you're not the only one who will pay a heavy price. Your relationships with loved ones will suffer. If you have children, you will be teaching them an unsustainable model for success. And you will never get that time back with your children or be able to "un-teach" them the lessons they've seen played out day after day, night after night, when they see you put work before everything—and everyone—else. Teach your children to respect your business and empower them to know what to do in critical situations, such as how to handle accidents, deal with people they don't feel safe with, and think their way through anything. You may think that right now you are simply surviving the chaos and confusion in your life. But you could be grooming future business owners and world changers. Don't lose your focus or your vision!

> ## Spiritual Takeaway
> I know that with faith all things are truly possible. No obstacle is insurmountable with Papa God.

CHAPTER 5

HE GETS ME

We all have a God-given need to be loved, accepted, and understood. Living our lives without those needs being met, as we were designed, is a recipe for problems. Believe me, I know from experience. The hands that were designed to love me caused pain instead. The people who should have taught me how accepted I was and how much I made Papa and others happy reminded me daily that I wasn't enough, was a bother, and they oftentimes joked about whether or not I was even a "real" member of the family. Being understood has been a rare thing for me. Feeling like someone who doesn't fit in and who will always be alone will make you someone who must self-protect (because no one else will protect you). At least that was my story, until I met the true, deep, accepting, kind, and understanding love of Papa God.

Sadly, this was not the experience of everyone I met in church. Many of the people on the church's payroll seemed to have a "calling" to make others feel inadequate and "lucky enough" to be saved by the grace of God. If I asked any questions, I was looked at as rebellious, disobedient, and combative. They expected submission. Especially from a woman. *Submissive*—that word was their constant sword. I wonder how many of you have had a similar experience?

When I began to see that Papa understands me, that He gets me, well, it changed everything. Then He began to lead me with this powerful statement: "Get into agreement with heaven."

To get into a mind-set and heart-turn of agreement with heaven changed everything. It brought out my true anomaly self because it went against everything I'd been taught. "Push ahead, strive, put your head down, and make it happen" is what we're told to do for success. But all of heaven was saying to me, "Get into agreement with us!"

A MESSAGE FROM PAPA'S HEART TO ALL OF US

I'll never forget the day He spoke to my heart and told me that I was fighting His goodness. Not only that, but I was also pushing away the love other people had for me and all of the wonderful things that were planned for my future. He then spoke these three words again over me, "Get into agreement." Little did I know that this would not only help me to heal, but it would also make me feel understood, worthy, and as though I had been created with everything I needed for my future. In the truest sense of the word, Papa understood me. He got me.

He gets you too. It's pretty incredible to think that we don't have to explain everything to Him. This concept alone would change our prayers, our focus, and our lives forever. To simply pause and meditate on the idea that, "The God of the Universe gets me," is transformational.

I vividly recall being in a church service, listening to the sermon and feeling like I was having an out-of-body experience. As the pastor spoke about God's disappointment in us, and how we can't push the love of God to its limits or we may encounter His wrath, I went to heaven in my heart and spoke to Papa about this. He was never like this with me. He had no limits. His love had no limits. I can remember times when in prayer He'd remind me that although I was "such a brat" sometimes, He would always love me and never abandon me as others had.

Abandonment fills the hearts of so many people I meet on a daily basis through my business, my social media channels, and even in the gym where I work out. Rejection and abandonment have left so many of us feeling like orphans. Our hearts cry out for fathers and mothers, yet we act as if we don't need anyone. If we believe that God will reject us anytime we fail, and will turn away from us whenever we make a mistake, this will breed distance, not the closeness we were designed for. I remember hearing the pastor say that if we went outside of the expectations that God so clearly had set up for us, we might end up finding ourselves in a place of no repair. "When the grace stops, we're in big trouble," he said. I checked out. The grace should have stopped a long, long time ago for me. Not only did I suffer horrific trauma throughout my life, but if I wrote down the mistakes I'd made, it would be a long list. The decisions that I made to go against what Papa was saying also created a long list.

A thought popped into my head: "We're in big trouble!"

"What does this mean anyway?" I argued back in my head. "Am I going to be struck dead by lightening? Will I suffer with horrific disease for the rest of my life? Will God make me lose everything that matters to me to teach me a lesson?" I had been taught many lessons by authorities in my life. Lessons that were actually horrific abuse by a predator. Was Papa now becoming a predator?

Just then, I felt that familiar warmth in my soul. The one that silences all of the false accusations, makes the doubt run far away, and reassures me that I am indeed never alone and should never fear being abandoned again. It was the voice of Papa God. It's a voice that is like no other and carries more weight that any person in authority I've ever met, yet is gentle, calm, peaceful, and makes me feel safe. "Papa knows me. He gets me. He sees the whole picture. He doesn't miss a detail, and He'll never ever leave me, forsake me, reject me, disown me, harm me, or manipulate me!" The truth rose up in my heart like a sword that could take on any giant that tried to raise its ugly head in my life!

The truth, once again, set me free.

GETTING INTO AGREEMENT WITH HEAVEN

I had a 24/7 relationship with Papa that was much more powerful than the time I spent in any church. Learning how to walk in these new faith shoes taught me more than I had even realized at the time. It gave me courage to do things I never would have done on my own. It brought the possibilities that I believed into life. But more than anything, it reminded me that I was created beautifully, powerfully, uniquely, differently, and specifically for a purpose. And all of heaven was cheering me on.

Grace never stops. The Bible teaches that where sin abounds, grace abounds even more. This doesn't mean we won't experience ramifications, but it means that Papa's love will always be true, will be there in our despair, will love us in our sin, and will never, ever run out, especially when we need it the most. So many people think God controls everything. That if good things happen, He did them. If bad things happen, He caused them. If He is so powerful, we should never suffer or struggle. This is ridiculous because it removes from the whole equation one very important aspect—free will. We are not puppets, wandering through the universe, subject to whatever the Great Owner of the Planet feels like doing. We were given power that nothing else on this planet possesses—free will. Animals don't have free will. Plants don't have free will. The sun doesn't get to rise whenever it feels like it, and the waves in the sea can't decide at any given moment when they'll let their tide rise and fall. No, all of these other things were set into motion and function in a way that is responding to everything around it. Environment is everything to all aspects of the planet. It is for us too, but we have a power that nothing else does. We get to choose. It's these choices—our choices, the choices of those who have gone before us and those who will follow after us—that are setting into motion many aspects of our existence.

Here's the big paradigm shift: we have both free will and the grace of God. We have a choice and we also receive what we didn't earn. We get what we didn't deserve. Papa is always for us and never against us, but life itself can at times kick us in the buttocks in a way that can throw us into a tailspin if we're not careful! This is why it's so critically important to know TRUTH. To find, and understand, and live in our truth.

As the pastor spoke of God's great disappointment in us and His mercy in not wiping us off the face of the planet, I felt sick. I felt violated. How could a powerful man of God speak such untruth, and why was he working so hard to make everyone in the congregation afraid of Papa? He has never, ever made me feel afraid of Him. I honor Him. I fear Him, in the biblical way, with a reverential honor and respect. But, even when He has had to deal with me about things that are really hard and really painful, He never takes a tone of abuse, sternness, or harshness. He's always patient, always loving, and it is THIS LOVE that caused me to trust Him. Fully and entirely I trust Him because I know who He is. This, here in this church, was religion and it was not the relationship I had with my Papa God. I know who He is and He knows me. This was not it!

Religion was sadly the greatest enemy I had ever encountered. It was showing up everywhere I went—trying to change me, remake me, put me into a box, or impose a boundary that was so scary it would literally destroy the relationship I had with Papa God, if I were to submit to it. This religious spirit shows up in the most unlikely of places. Not only is it infecting churches on a daily basis, it's weaving its way through bloodlines and misaligning and misinterpreting the message of love, forgiveness, and grace. It's based on all that we do instead of all that Papa has done. It's a system of earning and losing. But the gospel is a story of giving, restoring, and healing. Papa SO LOVED the world that He gave His only son. He didn't come into the world to condemn the world; He came so that we might be saved through Him. That was truth, not this terroristic, predatory nightmare that was causing people to not only run away from Him, but to run away from close relationships, intimacy, and community—all the things we were created for.

FINDING MY TRUEST SELF

Courage beyond anything I've ever known arose within me at this time in my life. I remember worshipping in church, when what I really longed for was to dance boldly and passionately before the Lord. I remember feeling like I'd rather be with a bunch of pagans seeking Papa than the unbelieving Christians I was around. At least these so-called pagans would be seeking Papa with an open heart and not handing out a to-do list in order to be accepted.

The power of faith in the most difficult seasons of life has not only proven to save my life over and over again, but it gave me courage beyond myself. When everyone else didn't understand me, this one thing anchored me, grounded me, and helped me to get back up, every morning. GOD LOVES ME. He gets me. All of heaven is cheering me on, and my job is to get into *agreement* with this truth.

That's a powerful thing. You know what it feels like when a friend "gets you." There's no long dialogue, no need to explain, disclaim, and make sure all the details are right. One look and they . . . get you. That's what I had in my relationship with Papa, but sadly, I never found it in the typical religion preached in most churches. In my darkest hour, I could look to Him and find that He'd be there. He'd be there in my mess and He'd be there in my victory. He always reminded me who I was, who I *truly* was. The warmth of Papa's love and smile could make me feel like I was born again, every single day. There was never a day that I couldn't start over, do better, renew and restore, and rise up again. He gave me hope that was far, far beyond just coping skills. In His eyes I saw the reflection of who I really was.

If I were to sum up the calling on my life, and the "ministry" that I've been called to in business and in life, that would be it. To remind people of Papa's great love for them so that they can remember *who* they are. This love will shine into all the darkest places. Hope will be found in hopeless places. All of the broken pieces will be put back together. This is the miraculous, wonderful, deep, deep love of God's heart. It takes just a second for Papa to fix things, and if we get into agreement with heaven on a daily basis and live a mind-set that is far removed and different than the rest of the world—an anomaly mind-set—this will become our new normal.

Faith is the substance of things unseen. Social media gave me an outlet to share my story and how I overcame trauma, and it became my go-to place for business as well. It became a place where faith took on substance.

When we look at the statement "Get into agreement with heaven," it might stir up some of the other agreements we've made in life. We agree to do our best when the challenges come. We agree to have and to hold, until death do us part when we marry. We agree to make our house payment on time, because if we don't pay, we can't stay! However, it's the untold, quiet agreements we don't talk about that are, quite frankly, screwing us up! Many times, we don't even realize we're making them. These agreements are forming, creating, and even controlling our lives. Then when we hear religion raise its ugly voice, we start making agreements that are in direct opposition to who we really are. We agree to hate ourselves every time we see someone who is different than we are, and who appears to have it all together while we're falling apart. We agree to find our self-worth in our work and to follow the path of enough is never enough.

Every time we silently say, "I'll never do that again!" we make an agreement.

Going through a lot of healing in the last ten years and sharing some of that with my followers on social media and the students in my academy, I've discovered that my struggles are my readers' struggles, and my pain they have also felt. This is why we are so connected. My innovative way of doing social media and marketing gave me a supernatural PUSH into all that I was to become, and it changed millions of people's lives as well. Maybe you are like me. We can oftentimes be our own worst enemy. I can take things that are good for me, and stretch them to the millionth degree, right to the point where the good becomes a tool of destruction. Learning to heal, forgive, let go, identify, break away, cut off, and rebuild are all great tools! It seems every little thing that happens in life must now be scrutinized, accessed, dissected, and prayed about. This is that sickening spirit of religion again! If we aren't careful we'll think that digestive upset from overindulging on lasagna, chocolate chip cookies, and wine is an attack from hell that needs deliverance, and all we really need is some enzymes to help.

What if there was an easier way to clear things up in our lives and in the spiritual realm? What if we could get clear, stay strong, and RESET in just a matter of seconds, anytime we needed to throughout the day? We can. It starts with getting into agreement with heaven.

We can get into agreement with heaven in our relationships, our health, our attitude, our hormones, our weight loss (YES!), and while raising our children, navigating through rush hour traffic, building our business, advancing in our career, and even in making decisions of where to live. What is heaven saying today? "Let's get into agreement!" That's the key.

WHAT IS HEAVEN?

Heaven has been depicted in so many ways is it any wonder so many people question whether or not it's even real? From the movie *Star Wars* to the Bible, galaxies, stars, the clouds, the place where Papa lives, where only good people go—heaven has a unique definition and picture in the mind of every one of us. Whatever we were raised with, taught, or exposed to, and even the things we caught through media, others, subtle impressions, and even big misunderstandings, heaven means something to us. Maybe it's a place you could never go to because you've had religion shame you and shape your beliefs. I get that.

You have felt like you aren't good enough, smart enough, and for crying out loud, you definitely aren't holy enough! Heaven has no interest in people like you. Imagine trying to "get into agreement" with these thoughts. Or maybe you believed that heaven was some fictitious, faraway place too lofty for earthly beings to comprehend. The place of angels and rainbows, where all of the tears are finally wiped away—but for now, you have to suffer, struggle, and hope you get out of this life alive. You've seen paintings of angels and looked up at the stars at night. Every day you do your best to love your fellow man, but the idea that heaven has any personal interest in you? Such words are too high to comprehend. Or you find reasons on a daily basis why you don't qualify, won't even try anymore, and, possibly, gave up years ago. If we think we're going to change our lives getting into agreement with something so far away, impersonal, and fairytale-ish, we'll just put fuel on the lies that religion has been spewing most of our lives. How do you turn to a mystery in the middle of your darkest night? Chasing fantasies is great when you're sitting on the porch of your white picket fence house sipping perfectly fresh-squeezed lemonade as you ponder all the things that make life grand . . . but when the curtain on this dream closes, and your "lemonade packet that you just added water to" life doesn't even compare, where do we go from here? It's all you know. It's all you've ever known. How do you get into agreement with that?

REMEMBER WHO YOU ARE

What if everything we've ever known or thought about heaven and Papa are very different? That's where the change begins. If religion has been poisoning the message of heaven for thousands of years, what if we invent the possibility that the longings of our hearts actually reveal that which we were made for? The desire to be loved, accepted, understood, trusted, and depended on are the longings of God's heart for us that were knit into each of our DNA strands. We have to learn to look beyond where we are today and gain a wider perspective, inviting Holy Spirit into everything that concerns us.

Here's the reality. Those of us who are called to do big things in the world are going to have to break the rules. You are designed to break the rules. You were created to go against the flow. Inside our DNA is a desire to break free, deviate from that which is typical, and rise above. This craving for more isn't greed, lust, or ungratefulness. It's a yearning, a divine, God-given yearning to fly above all that we know, have known, and could know into a realm that is beyond us! The world needs us to break the rules and to get into agreement with heaven. A lot of business owners and people I come in contact with tell me that their ability to break the rules got them into trouble at first. The thing inside of them that wants to buck the system, break free, and think on their own may have even gotten them punished when they were young or just starting out in their business. It can take just one more setback, one more stumble or slap on the wrist for thinking big that makes people start thinking small again. Then the questions start coming up again in their head, putting them back into the box of all that is called and seen as "normal." "Who are you? What makes you think *you* can do this?"

Well, what makes you think you *can't* do this?

Is this really a fear of success as we've thought all along, or is this a war in our head and our heart that is rooted in a fear of rejection of our success? We go from dreaming to fearing rejection, and before we know it, we put our dreams away, we get up in the morning to everything we've ever known, and we succumb to the pressure of just doing life as usual, even if it sucks, and even if we know there must be something more. God's purpose for our lives becomes something we journal about but not something we could ever comprehend actually living.

In the darkest hours of my despair when my business goals, dreams of success, and my history of pushing people away and hiding in my own prison got worse, I found that turning to Papa resolved the fear of rejection. Rather than telling Him all about it, reliving it, re-feeling it, and reopening the wound because of how far removed I felt from my dreams, I'd just sit quietly and remind myself of this one extremely powerful truth: "You get me. I need help." Thoughts of other people struggling came to my mind. Pictures of the single dad struggling to make ends meet, making a steadfast commitment to being a good leader and provider but weeping into his pillow at night so his children couldn't hear him, filled my mind. I could feel his weariness, his struggle, the war to want to play victim but the decision to be victorious. Or the wife who felt like she was a widow inside her marriage. The fact that her husband physically lived in the house didn't mean a thing, because he was beyond distant, and in a way he had abandoned the family. Neglect and fear were her breakfast daily. Crying in her car on the way to work and then making a decision to never give up, believe in more, and trust that Papa would change her life were in my mind like a movie reel. Thoughts of the teenager who wanted to be strong but took drugs in order to tune out the pain for just a few minutes bombarded my mind. The young girl who yearned for affection, safety, and security, and who was instead sexually molested every single morning for years, haunted me. Maybe these are your stories. As I cried out to Papa to give me courage and to help me to not quit, my focus grew beyond my own fears and insecurities and a warrior-like power would surge through my veins. "Not today!" I'd declare and fight one more day for all that I knew was truth for me. And for others.

ENDURE

My preventative plan for derailing my enemy and the lies of rejection was to spend time with Papa before anyone else woke up and to invite Him into everything concerning me. When I would do this, a strength beyond myself rose up and an interception with heaven would take place. It's hard to describe, but it was like being fueled with supernatural energy while having clarity that was beyond a cloudless day. It felt as though it was literally surging through my veins. My DNA would change, my mind would open, and my soul would get into agreement and alignment with all that I was made for. I'd *remember* who I was!

When you start breaking the rules enough, "the system" will make room for you. They have to. The anomalies, unicorns, and revolutionaries of the world have changed things for all of us! I'm reminded of a scene in the movie *Braveheart* that will forever be imprinted in my mind. Mel Gibson, playing the character of

William Wallace, is strapped into a torture device, and they are literally stretching his body until his tendons break. They then get ready to dig into his bowels to rip his insides out. Right there. Right then . . . he screams at the top of his lungs, as all of the city watches, "FREEEEEEEEEEEEEEDOM!" Maybe you've seen this movie, and felt that warrior anomaly fire rise up inside of you to fight to the death for all you've been made for!

To be brave is to be willing to be courageous in the face of danger or difficulty. It means to endure. Our hearts must be brave hearts to endure what we've been called to! This is why we need each other and we can't be silent any longer. We must pray for God to give us courage to break the rules and to fight hard on the battlefield of our lives to break all the delusions, lies, and religion and to find the truth that Papa God created us for!

When you do this, when you start and end each day and each battle with Papa, then a beautiful thing happens. When you do that with all the courage God gives you, you encourage someone else. This is a foundational part of my job: to use the courage Papa gives me to encourage others.

BIG-PICTURE LESSON

Wherever you are now, please know that today is not the end. This thing you thought would destroy you, will not. By learning to look beyond today and gain a wider perspective, while also inviting Papa's Heart and Spirit into everything you do, you will find that your New Constant Companion will provide answers in an instant when you need them; He can shift things you can't even understand and connect you to a life we were made for, even in difficulty, and especially in pain. Believe me, I know it takes courage when you don't fit in. Within that pain of trying to belong, who you really are is revealed. And you will see that Papa made you perfect. He made you complete. You lack nothing. And the supernatural blessing Papa God has is coming, and all you have to do is be your beautiful anomaly self.

ANOMALY ACTION: COURAGE BEYOND YOURSELF

People often ask me if there are steps that I take daily that have contributed to my success. I'm humbled by the question. And the answer is yes. There are seven things I do daily beyond my morning routine that frame my day and my mind for success. They have been life-changing for me, and can be for you as well:

1. **Get into agreement with heaven.** The Passion Translation of the verse Romans 4:5 of the Bible says this: "But no one earns God's righteousness. It can only be transferred when we no longer rely on our own works, but believe in the One who powerfully declares the ungodly to be righteous in His eyes. It is faith that transfers God's righteousness into our account." FAITH puts a deposit into our lives, DNA, and potential with things that we didn't earn or learn on our own, but for which we were made for. When we get into agreement with Papa and heaven, we lay aside our own pain as a victim and choose to be victorious and strong! We go from being victims to being someone who was victimized but who overcame adversity and turned the pain into a sword.

2. **Make a decision to do what has never been done.** We can't keep living life like everyone else and expect to have some kind of different result. This might mean we have to relocate, put up better boundaries, and dismantle all the old ways of thinking and being that we were so accustomed to. It's time we invent possibility where walls existed. Co-create what we want with Papa God rather than believing that this is just how things have always been, always will be, and we might as well get used to it.

3. **Say out loud the kind of things you want to see in your day.** Neuroplasticity means that the brain listens to our words. Say what you want. Stop focusing on all the things you don't want, are afraid of, and hope don't happen! Speak aloud what you want to see. Declare it to be so and then believe it with everything you have. Effort is your personal responsibility. Heaven will take care of the miracles.

4. **Visualize your goals.** Send pictures to your brain of what you want. Lay down for a few moments every single day. Allow

your body to be perfectly still. Release all the tension, stress, self-defense, worries, and fear. See the thing you want as if it's already been done. Feel the satisfaction, the accomplishment, the joy and celebration. Start sending these signals to your brain daily, and watch as supernatural things become your new normal.

5. Take one step daily toward your goal. Things won't change overnight, but many days and nights added together will get you to your goal. Every single baby step forward is an accomplishment, so to stay focused even when you want to give up is victory. Especially when you want to give up! Write things down in a journal that you can review as you're going forward. You must get really good at being your own voice of encouragement. People may never understand you, be able to relate to you, or quite "get" you; but always remember that God does get you, and your goal is to get into agreement with heaven, not to please other people. Years from now you'll be reading through your journal, and in your journey you'll find keys to help others. So just take one step at a time and have faith that you will get there. You WILL get there.

6. Be willing to be the different one. The one thing that no one else has is *you*. Your voice, story, heart, soul, ambition, focus, message, feelings, love, light, and life. That's all yours. It was the gift Papa gave you. Be willing to stand alone. Be willing to go forward so that others may follow. If we want to live like no one else ever has and make a difference in the lives of many people, we must be willing to carry the baton alone. Papa God is the only One who can set our souls free. He is the One who reminds us who we are. In this space, where you are alone, being different, remember, you're never alone. All of heaven is cheering you on!

7. Embrace the process. Some aspects and parts of your journey will not be pretty, nor will they be pain free. But when we keep the first thing first—getting into agreement with heaven—and we hang on to every word that Papa God speaks over us, rather than the lies the enemy throws at us, we'll go places that seemed possible only in our dreams. Every twist, turn, and move gets you closer. The process might not make any sense at all, but trust it.

Embrace it. Be willing to travel the road that no one else will, so that you can carry that flag of victory that is meant for you!

Grab a Journal!

Have you ever felt like you were completely understood by one person? If you have, or even if you haven't, write out the things that you feel are the most difficult to understand about who you are. What are the down, dirty, most hidden parts of your heart that no one ever gets to see? Write it down. Let Papa see. He already knows anyway. Open your heart to love. Open your heart to life and light!

RESISTANCE: CHANGE THE CHANNEL OF THE VOICE IN YOUR HEAD

The thoughts you are taking in early in the morning—the things you are uploading into your brain by what you expose yourself to—these will inform and direct your day. The Anomaly Action I shared earlier will give you powerful tools against resistance every day. I wake up and consciously say, "It's going to be a fantastic day! All of heaven is cheering me on." When you do this you are telling your brain how to think. But, of course, resistance gets up as early as I do!

So there is a thought that pops up that pushes back. "Wait, what's all that positive self-talk? This is going to be a rotten day. Don't be such a Pollyanna—all that positivity is useless." That's the voice from hell. It lies to you. And if you put lies into your brain, it will hold on to them. *So shift your state, people!*

If you thought you were dealing with the pinnacle of resistance before, think again. This is where the WAR gets real. Will we continue to strive, push, and force things all on our own, hoping to control everything, or will we learn to walk by faith with God into the darkness, knowing that He is the light?

Stand strong! Say to that voice of negativity, "Yes, putting positive information out there is going to change everything for me. It will be a great day. I'm going to be stronger than I was yesterday." Then see yourself succeeding. Take some baby steps away from resistance. This negative programming didn't happen overnight, so changing it will take time. In order to combat this negative messaging in my brain, I change the channel. I have affirmations all over the place. There is the sound of worship music going all the time in my house. Do negative things happen? Sure. But I don't let them take me down. I take a deep breath and stay in control over how I respond.

So when resistance comes, do a course correction. Nothing is worth you missing out on the blessed plan that the entire universe and all of heaven has for you.

> ### Spiritual Takeaway
> I will look into the mirror of Papa's love and see myself as He sees me: beautiful, powerful, and loved beyond measure.

CHAPTER 6

THE SPIRITUAL UNICORN

I am a Unicorn. I know this about myself and I embrace it. However, common citizens of planet Earth are not accustomed to unicorns invading their territory. They see the bright colors—my pink hair like a horn coming out of my head and pointing the way—and they have a lot of different reactions. Some are amused, others are filled with questions, and still others are intrigued and watch from a distance. But over and over again the common thing I hear from millions of followers on social media is this: Sandi, *you* give me courage to be who I am meant to be. Imagine that. The war I've fought was not just about me and my freedom. Finding my truth was just the birthing ground for many others to connect to. Your journey and story is also a birthing ground. This is why it can feel so painful. Birth is never easy. We pass from one realm to another and encounter opposition.

An anomaly must think differently than most people to rise to levels that are beyond anything they've ever experienced before. The battle between trying to be all things to all people and losing yourself like a chameleon will lead to finding out what you were made for and why this war began in the first place.

Through all my challenges, weaknesses, and struggles, the truth that would set me free was that *Papa God* made me to be a unicorn, and if I were to embrace this, a brave new world would open up to me. But my world wasn't always brave, it was terrifying. My ability to embrace my uniqueness didn't happen overnight, I tried wearing everyone else's identities for me for a long, long time. But pictures of heaven, and the places I've been with Papa began to fill my mind to remind me that I was definitely not of this world. Passing through was my mission. My purpose was not to plant my tent pegs deeply and become like others, it was to transform cultures and to bring freedom to those who hide in darkness. I know, because hiding in darkness myself for so many years gave me an unusual advantage where my enemy was concerned—I knew his tricks. Little did he know that I have been to heaven a few times, and not because I died. No, in my prayer times, I've literally been taken to a world I've never seen before to encounter things that no person on earth has yet to experience.

VISITING HEAVEN

There is a business room in heaven. I've been there. One day I was on my office floor crying out to God for grace for my day, and I fell into what felt like sleep, though I was still fully awake. In the movie reel in my mind I began to see golden steps. Papa said, "Let's climb higher." So, I did. We were taken to a massive gold door that was guarded on both sides by huge angels. They looked like half men, half angelic beings, and I could literally feel their power as I walked closer. But they didn't guard or prevent me from walking through the massive gold door. Instead, they opened it for me and waved me through. WHOA. I know. Keep reading.

Once inside, the room expanded as I stepped forward. It was like my steps made the walls go wider and the depth grow instantly. Then I saw maps, gold maps, of the entire world. There were file cabinets, wall hangings, and bookcases with thousands and thousands of gold books! I touched gently the things around me and felt authority, wisdom, and power rush through my veins as my human fingers touched heavenly items. Papa spoke. "This is the business room of innovation, recreation, ideas, and wonders. It is here that dreams are made and supplied. We have all things pertaining to life and business. Those who will believe can receive, freely."

I think I was so overwhelmed with what was just said that my heavenly visitation ended in a flash and I was on my office room floor again sobbing and shaking until I felt like I'd cry my insides out. "What the HECK was THAT!" I thought. "It felt so safe and holy and God loves me, and He's always loved me, and He'll never leave me, and everything I know is just the beginning, and there is no end, and how on earth do I tell anyone about this, and what should I do now?" All this ran through my head.

I heard Papa again. "Breathe. I'll bring it to you when you need it.

SUPERNATURAL LOVE

So . . . hopefully you're still reading. Maybe you're thinking, *She's a Unicorn, she's been to heaven, and Papa God, as she calls Him, speaks to her about things in heaven.* Some of you are sobbing, because you've been there too and had no idea what it was. Some of you are crying and shaking because you just felt life go through your veins in a way that you've never ever experienced before. You're touching this book in your hands, and looking at it like it's a cross between that game in the movie *Jumanji* come to life craziness and Wisdom of the Ages information that has just been translated. Where do we go from *here*?

A lot of traditional Christians will have a really hard time with what I just shared. They don't believe in the sign gifts anymore; have obliterated the prophets, apostles, and healers out of the church; and are trying to lead people with the five-fold ministry turned into two bad guys called the pastor and the teacher. So they have no room in their theological tenants for this kind of talk! And there are other Christians who have been encountering the supernatural love and the heart of Papa for years in their closet who are too scared out of their wits to even talk about it. And now I've just opened the door and told the entire world what they've been experiencing. Where do we go from here, indeed? We'll hear from new agers and even people who don't consider themselves religious or spiritual who are encountering similar things and had no clue it was heaven.

I'll tell you where we go from here.

We should probably continue lying on the floor for a while in shock. Then we can thank Papa for sharing such incredible things with us. Now we should ask Him to keep us, protect us, and help us to do the next thing, whatever it is that He desires for our lives.

Maybe you've never had such an experience but you've been breaking rules, being resourceful, and doing things on your own for most of your life. I'm here to provoke you to think through the things you hide from others that have sustained you. They could be the answers you've been waiting and praying for!

THE WAY OF THE UNICORN

Here's a story I've shared in my business trainings and it's changed a lot of parents' and entrepreneurs' ways of walking in faith. I believe it will help you. It was birthed out of my own encounters in heaven.

As I homeschooled my children, one of the greatest things I ever taught them was that they were all created uniquely, powerfully, and individually. I wish with all of my heart we all had that teaching in our lives. My "curriculum" was very individual to their needs. Some of my sons loved to do math drills on paper or using the computer. I also had a son who wanted to do his math drills running up and down the stairs! Yes, one step, 1 times 1 equals 1. Next step, 1 times 2 equals 2. And so on. We did addition, subtraction, multiplication, and division up and down those stairs in our house! Or to be even more creative, upside down on a chair. He loved to sit with his feet in the air and his bottom upside down! Lord have mercy, thank God he outgrew that.

Because everything I did with Papa in life and in my business was done in a "unicorn way," I figured it wasn't going to hurt anyone to let my son do his math tables with activity! It proved to be the key that he needed for focus. Today, he's very calm and contemplative. But when he's stuck, he knows that movement is his door to more creativity. My unicorn ways opened many doors for my sons. And for me. They've also opened doors for multiple business owners who tried doing things according to how the experts have instructed for years, and it has never worked! I'm here to say, "You were meant to walk through these doors!"

When we learn to embrace our individuality and uniqueness, it's not something we have to reject or adapt to. The choice to NOT fit in and to explore the truth of who we really are, can turn us into an unstoppable force as we help others to be who they were made to be as well. The unicorns are in the same boat as the extremely analytical genius who must wear the same color shirt 365 days per year so he or she doesn't have to think about clothing and instead can focus on the more important things in day-to-day life. Not all anomalies look different. Some of you will never stand out in a mall, but if we were to peek inside your brain and into how you think, we'd see something very different and unique. Papa has set this in motion in a very strategic way!

BECOMING WHOLE

So let me ask you something. Why do we try to change other people when we realize *we* don't fit in? It's crucial to remember that we don't need anyone to do anything, to undo anything, to say or become *anything* for us to be free. It's our birthright to live in freedom, and it's 100 percent dependent on whether or not we'll embrace who we are and be willing to shine even more as the darkness increases. Please, don't lose heart!

We need to be the biggest cheerleaders possible when it comes to the people in our lives, rather than the biggest critics. The very things we struggle with and fight will become the things we'll judge, attack, and criticize in others if we don't become whole. Because being an anomaly uses up enormous amounts of energy, self-care is crucial for us. The minute we neglect self-care, we start feeling jealousy, doubt, fear, and a bunch of other things that are so contrary to who we *really* are! You and I were not created with these things. Self-care is a huge key to abolishing them from our life and our DNA. Since we know the body keeps record of how we feel, act, and believe, it's even more important to build a strong foundation in our DNA so that our body can produce and bring forth what we truly want!

When my sons were little, my way of managing my home, running a company, and homeschooling them worked. They were growing, we were thriving together, and my business had grown past a million dollars in profit. But the old self-doubt, which was still at the time written deep into my DNA, began to question if it was enough. Comparison to and jealousy of the lives of others nearly cannibalized my dreams. My marriage was in a very painful place, and as I look back, it might have helped if I had filed for a divorce sooner. But because of my religious beliefs and fear of the ramifications of standing on my own two feet in that area of my life, I wouldn't file for divorce until over 12 years later.

This fueled my self-doubt and pushed me into perfectionism. The lies grew very deep. If I could just work more, make more money, have the children always quiet and perfect, the house always clean, have energy abounding even when I was on immunosuppressant and pain meds, then finally my life would be happy, and I'd be loved. Some of you are crying right now because this is *your* life story. You're pushing, and striving, and trying to make things better so you don't have to suffer so much. When in reality, being yourself, loving yourself, and doing life in your own unique way is the path to freedom and power.

THE SHIFT

Living with a duality of mind, essentially a split spirit, can lead to physical pain, ulcers, and more. I was battling multiple autoimmune conditions, and the more I pressed into perfectionism, the sicker I got. Many years later I'd see that my happy, carefree, scheduled yet flexible nature would have healed so much for me *if* I had embraced it. It wasn't until I got to my end, and filed for a divorce in 2015, that I came face to face with the reality of who I had become. My children had grown, they no longer lived at home, and I was still striving, pressing forward, and trying to control everything so that I wouldn't be hurt. But when I received healing through a ministry that helped me to see that my denial of truth was killing me, things shifted *fast*. Embracing who Papa made me to be caused my body to begin healing, so I reached out for better doctors, got off all medication, went back to the gym, and found a brave, new, empowering unicorn life waiting for me.

Along the way I also discovered the power of self-care and the enormous strength in saying, "No." The key to learning how to say yes to things came by way of saying no to things that would hinder my self-care. I had gotten really good at saying no in my business, but when it came to self-care, I was the last one I was caring for. When this shifted, it was like an enormous black cloud was lifted off my mind, my body, and my soul.

Learning to be my truest unicorn self was a journey, but learning to love myself was a miracle.

Self-love had been such a foreign concept to me because of the religious upbringing I had. And the religious and theological training of self-hate for holiness quite frankly polluted my relationship with myself. I could memorize all the verses better than anyone on denying oneself, losing oneself, hating one's own life so that we might gain. It brings tears to my eyes as I think about it, the wounds that my own heart caused my soul. Or maybe it was my mind.

THE PATH TO SELF-LOVE

We create neural pathways and memories with everything we experience and encounter. Many of these don't actually grow, they fall off, and are no longer a part of our lives or our memory. At some point, whether the behavior is learned or decided, we reject things, we won't let ourselves attach to them, and the branches in our memory and DNA are overwritten or eliminated. Now listen to this—this act of not allowing something to "take root" and "shedding" the memory out of our neural pathways can happen with things we should reject, but it can also happen with things we should have received.

We can teach ourselves to reject love, affection, and connection. We can get to the point where our subconscious mind disassociates and dislodges the memories from our brain's pathways even when it might have been the best thing for us, for life and health! I know because I was there. With good things and with things that should have been rejected. When I began to remove trauma from my muscles, my neural pathways, and my memory, things shifted. By overwriting pain with love, and forgiveness and belief in the person Papa God made me to be, the hypervigilant state in which I lived in began to fade. It was like losing an addiction to a substance that was killing me. For me? My substance was anxiety and panic. So many things triggered and set me off. Running away, rejecting love, and abandoning myself became a part of who I was without even thinking. When Papa began to heal me, all the feelings I began to experience were very overwhelming.

Loneliness, abandonment, and the pain of rejection were imbedded so deeply in my DNA that I became numb. When healing came, and my muscles were no longer screaming out in pain through inflammation, weakness, and swelling, my soul began to feel again. Oh, what a beautiful, completely out-of-control mess that can be! But since I could now feel the loneliness, the abandonment was right there at the surface, breaking my heart with rejection.

The first phase of healing was learning to feel again. The second phase was discerning and identifying truth. So when I started dating again, I had to accept that when my boyfriend didn't call when he said he would it was just because something else had come up. I had to be able to discern the difference between a simple mistake and an intentional slight. I realized it wasn't a passive-aggressive, predatorial way of abandoning and rejecting me like what had happened to me in my past! But it felt like it initially. When people began to question me about things at work, or in our relationships, and were brave enough to tell me the truth if I said something hurtful, a loneliness and desire to run and hide were so great I thought I'd have a nervous breakdown! *But it wasn't real.* It was the *feeling* of loneliness. It was the *mirror* of abandonment and the *memory* of rejection. As soon as my mind and body knew this as truth, and Papa walked into those rooms of my heart, everything shifted. I could now talk about how I was feeling, and the people around me started loving me even more because of my transparency. My boyfriend grew even more protective and patient with me when he realized he hadn't done anything, that my body and soul were healing, and it was his honor to love me through it all. He had such a deep capacity to love, only Papa could have brought a man like that into my life during those times.

Walking through these things brought me face to face with the truth of self-care and the neglectful habits I'd had in that realm. I was back at the gym, having massages, allowing myself to enjoy the sunshine, taking naps if I needed it—but none of it had been a part of my *lifestyle* until a decision was made.

BIG-PICTURE LESSON

I started out this chapter saying that I am a unicorn. Some of you chuckled. Some of you shook your head and thought, *Ummmm, unicorns aren't real, so are you saying you aren't real?* As I've told you about my journey to finding my truest self, you might be wondering why I'd call myself a unicorn. Because if I called myself an anomaly you might have had to look it up in the dictionary online. Some of you would have questioned the definition of deviating from that which is normal. You knew just what I meant, though, when I said I referred to myself as a legendary creature from faraway lands who brings healing and has magical powers. While I don't have magical powers and I did come from the planet Earth just like all of you, my journey has been extreme. It was horrific in a lot of ways. To tell the whole story would take another full book and a movie script! So Papa took me to a faraway land in heaven called "Love Rescue Inn." He poured reckless, abundant, and crazy love all over my wounds. He fought for me when despair and lack of love tried to destroy me. When I felt like I was worthless, He took care of the cost and paid it all. His kindness leaked into my DNA. His goodness spread through my system like a virus gone wild. It was this journey of love and restoration that has brought me to where I am today. It's quite scandalous really. It's beyond magical. It's supernatural. It's divine. It's what I was made for, and it's what you were made for too. So, embrace your inner unicorn. And reveal how truly strong and powerful you are.

ANOMALY ACTION: SELF-CARE STEPS TOWARD HEALING

I'd like to share with you a few things that helped me through my identification and healing process. It's my prayer that you will find yourself, buried inside of your DNA, shining back at you in the reflection of your Heavenly Father, and that you will know that you are good, you are powerful, and you were designed and created perfectly! Healing is a *huge* key to success in business. Our business will reflect our lives and our soul. Do the work to heal yourself—you are the greatest asset you have!

Give yourself time. I've lived through what seems like three lifetimes. No one should ever have to go through the pain and suffering I did. The trauma was rooted deeply into my DNA from the womb until I was in my 50s. Thankfully it didn't take 50 years to heal, but it did take a few years. Things started in a miraculous, powerful way in 2014 and would hit an all-time high in 2017 when I moved to Arizona. It was the year I weaned off all opiates, let go of all anti-inflammatories, said no to toxic relationships, got the right people onboard in my company, and really began to heal. To some people, walking through three or four years of healing can sound like forever. But if you've been suffering forever, it will seem like a very small price and a short time to walk through. Give yourself the time to heal. Make it a priority in your life.

Get the medical and spiritual care you *deserve*. Please stop using lack of money, poor location, or time as an excuse to stay stuck and suffering in old identities. If relocating, downsizing, selling things you own, and changing your lifestyle means that you can now get the best care for yourself, DO IT. Stop putting yourself off. Self-care means you come first. Have your hormones checked. See a naturopath. Study alternative methods, and be willing to give it your all. This is your life we're talking about, not a weekend project.

Learn how to use scientific breakthroughs to help improve your thinking, overcome past trauma, keep yourself mentally young and sharp, and grow new positive neurons in your brain that support the unicorn you truly are. Neuroplasticity is why it is possible to reprogram and restore yourself to your truest identity at any age, or on any part of your journey. You can literally rewire your brain for success. Being your truest self will be the most invigorating, empowering thing you will ever embark on!

Get spiritual help. For me that came through a ministry called Restoring the Foundations. Not only was it a gateway to healing for me, but it literally became a treasure chest of powerful living tools that helped me take back all that was stolen and walk in all that I was given! Learn more at www.rtfi.org.

Learn more about yourself. The numerous tests I've taken trying to figure out my personality, strengths, weaknesses, spiritual gifts, and more led me to one test that I recommend to all my students and use personally. It's called the Kolbe Test and is based on instincts. (You can get more information at www.arealchange.com/kolbe.) My test showed me that I had been divinely wired for the things I loved in my career and my life. Copywriter, marketer, talk show host, therapist, and more resonated so deeply with who I was. The modality in which I operated in these gifts was also revealed. My "quick start" and "fact finding only for a reason" nature was found on the pages of this program. I also discovered why I love to do group coaching, live events, and in-person seminars more than one-on-one private consulting on the phone. It explained why I felt physically sick having to repeat and reteach things over and over again. It also showed me how to keep my energy high and use my quick-start nature as an advantage in a world that was moving at an excruciatingly slow pace.

Grab a Journal!

Where do you need healing? Have you been trying to fit in and accommodate people around you? How long has this habit been going on? Find the cracks. Be brave. Feel safe. Write it down. Find the broken places that love and light need to heal. Let the pages of your journal begin the journey to your best self.

RESISTANCE: DON'T BE DIMINISHED

The system seeks to destroy and torment those who walk alone. So it can be lonely to be a unicorn. Believe me, I know. The yearning to belong seems to require that we diminish our true identities in order to fit into expected roles.

Right now, wherever you are, imagine yourself becoming smaller in order to fit into a tight, confining space. Do you feel powerful? Like you could change the world? No doubt you feel restricted. Confined. But maybe this feels familiar. I'm not surprised. Resistance sometimes disguises itself as conformity. But reducing yourself in order to fit in is a trap. Don't be fooled. Resistance wants you to play small. You don't have to let it. None of us do. Instead of making ourselves smaller so we don't stand out, we should instead expand ourselves greatly and confidently into the divine destiny God has chosen for us. It is what we are meant to do.

Like a unicorn, you will stand out. After all, a unicorn can never reshape itself into a horse. Yet as an anomaly, you may have spent your whole life trying to reshape yourself into something you are not in order to fit in. And when you try, you may find yourself paying a heavy price with your health and your emotional well-being. Resistance for "unicorns" may come in the form of persistent health issues. Stomach pain. Headaches. Feelings of unease and restlessness.

So, what if you stopped trying to be someone you are not? There is room in a loving world for each of us to belong to the human family, all of us created by Papa God with a unique purpose.

Let go of the need to fit *in* and embrace your soul's desire to stand *out*.

Sure, you'll get pushback from the people in your life who feel threatened by the expression of your true self. They will doubt you. Let them. They will try and discourage you. Ignore them. They will stop believing in you. Believe in yourself.

You are a unicorn after all.

> ## Spiritual Takeaway
> I am powerful, unique, and incredibly well made for this generation and this season.

CHAPTER 7

THE FRAUD POLICE

The first time I ever met the fraud police was when I was in high school. I loved to sing and play the guitar. It was a creative outlet for me, and had always been a way for me to express myself. The first time I played I was in the third grade. My parents got me lessons initially, and then I just flew past all of the instruction and began playing songs by ear. My ability to transpose sounds into my fingers and play the melodies, even if I didn't know the chord names, was a real gift. But my inability to read music, or to understand music theory, made me question myself.

"Do you even know how to play? Why are you doing this? You can't even read music! What if they find out? You're going to make a fool of yourself and everyone will know," said the voices racing through my head.

The fraud police and the "who do you think you are" community of condemnation and doubt seemed to rear their ugly heads whenever I would do anything that showed my talent. Singing was one skill that was attacked in a big way. As I look back now, I'm not sure if people were threatened by me or if I was threatened by my own incredible light. Probably a mix of both.

It was a beautiful fall Sunday and excitement was in my heart! Leading worship was something I loved to do so much. Singing and praising Papa God, and inviting others to open their heart and spirit to His love filled me with grace and courage like very few other things could. Even now, my most favorite thing to do in this life is talk to Papa and sing to and with Him.

As I scurried through the kitchen, making breakfast for my kiddos, getting things ready for our family to leave, the familiar yet painful voices started. But this time it came from a family member. "Why do you sing anyway? To show off and make people pay attention to you?" The tears welled up in my eyes, and my throat started to close up as I held back the emotions. As I swallowed down my pain and acted as if I hadn't heard what was said, I realized that the fraud police were now using people very close to me to destroy my dreams.

It's not like the words were meant to intentionally hurt me, but the enemy used the pain to try to stop me, to make me reconsider and doubt who I was and what I was doing. It was like a knife that the enemy wanted to send through my entire life, and he got as close as he could to insert his fatal blows.

It's been more than 14 years since I've lead worship or sang in church. Or any public place for that matter. The pain got too great, the voices too loud, and the fraud police took me to prison. Has this happened to you too?

We are given a gift or talent, a dream, and a blessing to share with the world, and our first encounter with opposition comes with these questioning words:

"WHO do YOU think you are? You can't do that. You're not different than us. You're just like us. If you do that you'll make us feel inadequate or unable or incapable, and that won't be fair, so you need to stop now and just be like us. Become mediocre. Don't get your hopes up too high, because all you'll do is get your feelings hurt and dreams crushed."

This chatter is like an anti-dream terrorist organization that most of us will encounter as we even think, let alone attempt, to do great things. As I've talked to people all over the world in our classes, at our events, through private consulting, and on my social media channels, I've learned that the fraud police know no boundaries or borders. They show up no matter who you are, what your background is, or what your skin color, gender, income bracket, worldview, or country! How on earth is this possible? I've often wondered if it is indeed an evil force sent to destroy us, or wiring in our brains that misfires when we attempt to do great things.

That wouldn't make any sense, though. If we are fearfully and wonderfully, intelligently and uniquely made by a God who loves us, why would there be any faulty setup in our hardware? In other words, how could we all be wired with something internal that sets out to destroy us? Neuroscientists have shown that we decide if someone is trustworthy as fast as our eyes blink. One blink—nope, you're danger. One blink—nope, you're suspicious. One blink—yes, I can trust you. Another thing we've discovered through the study of neuroplasticity and how the mind-body heals itself is the power of what we say when we talk to ourselves. Could it be that we are given this enormous capacity to be greater than ourselves by a loving Father in heaven, but we as a human race have used this ability and capacity for self-destruction, loathing, and self-deprecating? So, we distrust our own selves in a blink and ultimately decide we're unworthy?

As I've grown in my pursuits of chasing the dreams Papa has given me, and expanding my capacity and growth as a person, it's become obvious that the fraud police never disappear. They are always there. In other words, this outside force, this enemy, or this internal destruction that we use against ourselves, never leaves no matter how successful we become and no matter how many battles we win. With this understanding, we can learn a few things that will help prepare us for this inevitable challenge.

FOCUS ON THE WORK AND NOT THE WORKER

It's my honor to lead over 2,500 small business owners every week in our virtual academy. We connect via a webinar format. Oftentimes, in our open Q&A sessions my students will bring their most challenging questions. This one comes up often: "How do I market myself without feeling arrogant or self-centered?" Do you see the fraud police showing up there? When Papa gives us a gift, talent, idea, business concept, ministry focus, music inspiration, book to write, or anything else we have to share with the world, WHY do we question whether it's a pure motive to get it out into the world or a selfish one? WHY do we put on religious cloaks to cover up our pure heart and wear self-imposed sackcloth and ashes to try to prove we're not being arrogant, when in reality, we're inspired, motivated, and even enthusiastic about sharing with the world our blessing so that they might be blessed too!

At the very root of the word, *enthusiasm* means to be IN GOD. "Entheos" is to be close, as one, in God. When we're excited and enthused about sharing what Papa gave us, we are doing a holy work, not a selfish one! Locking ourselves up in a cabin, building a shrine around ourselves, and isolating our gifts so that no one gets to benefit from our blessing is selfish and arrogant. Stepping past fear into courage and bringing that message and gift to the world through social media, a website, and even videos, is evidence of someone who is being selfless!

This has been one of the greatest lessons I've ever personally learned, and now I have the honor of imparting it to my students. The fraud police never shut up. But if we focus on the work more than the worker—if we obsess about the gift we're releasing to the world rather than if we're worthy enough, perfect enough, or "somebody" enough to have such a gift—we'll find joy in the struggle. We'll find purpose in our pain and grace to succeed!

NO COMPARISON

You've probably heard before that no one is like you. I'm sure deep in the recesses of your memory is the fact that your DNA is unique, and the probability of you even being here is miraculous! Did you know that the average man will send nearly 100 million sperm after one egg, and because of the defense mechanisms created around the egg, only a few hundred, if circumstances are ideal, will even get through? And only one will win! The reality is one sperm won the race of 100 million to the egg and then YOU were created. WOW. Why on earth would you ever compare yourself to other people? Crazy, isn't it?

There is no comparison, but deep inside our mainframe, inside our heart and spirit and mind, is a "programmed need" for acceptance and belonging. Sadly, at a very young age we begin to look outside the confines of our home and our parents, and we look to others for validation and belonging. This is when comparison begins. This is when it is so crucial to pay attention to what we are *saying* as we talk to ourselves! If only parents and schools could partner together to teach young people to say the right things to help their body, mind, and spirit to rise up to its capacity *rather* than resorting to the self-destruction of comparison.

> *"We compare ourselves among ourselves and prove*
> *only one thing—we're unwise." 2 Cor 10:12*

It is wise and even holy to realize there is no comparison when it comes to you and me. We're unique. We're anomalies, all of us. We're wired to need each other, but we're not wired to be exactly alike. A big key to learning how to deal with the fraud police is understanding how important it is to not compare yourself to anyone. Let your goals and challenge be driven by becoming a better person—yourself. Focus on how you can improve in being your most true, authentic self. This will silence the police in your head and give you courage to stand alone, in the midst of a crowd.

FORGIVENESS

Not many business books are written with a focus on forgiveness. Far too many spiritual books are written with a focus on forgiveness but don't bring it into the marketplace. The fraud police present a unique situation and opportunity. Can we forgive ourselves for all the times we gave in and didn't press forward? Can we forgive those around us who didn't realize they were being used to attempt to stop us? Can we forgive our competitors for only focusing on how to win and forgetting the value of individual growth?

To forgive means to stop feeling angry or resentful. It means to cancel a debt or feeling of indebtedness. Can we let go of the angry and resentful feelings that are rising up inside us, constantly questioning our worth, our intelligence, and our talent? Can we move forward and return to love in our growth and success, understanding that the fraud police will always be with us, and realize that we don't ever have to answer to them? That's where real change begins. The incredible power of ignoring the negative lies and challenging them with truth and love. This is where we'll truly find out WHO we really are and celebrate!

BIG-PICTURE LESSON

As you transcend the negative voice within and achieve success, you will find that money creates a magnifier that reveals not only your destiny but also the weaknesses and lies you are walking in. This reflection can take you to new levels if you are willing to really see who is in the mirror, rather than listening to the limiting voices in your head.

ANOMALY ACTION: FEAR OR FAITH?

In the following quiz, read one question at a time as quickly as possible. Don't deliberate or think about your responses. Respond honestly with your gut reaction by circling (A) or (B). Let's begin:

1. You've been asked to speak in front of 100 people in two weeks about a topic dear to your heart. Do you

   (A) decline or

   (B) accept?

2. A career opportunity arises for you to move across the country, requiring you to start fresh in a place where you don't know anyone. Do you

(A) stay put or

(B) pick up and move, knowing a chance like this may never come again?

3. A co-worker invites you to join a company team, but you would be playing a sport you're not good at. Do you

(A) make an excuse about why you won't be able to play or

(B) embrace the opportunity to learn from other colleagues with more knowledge of the game?

4. You're in a long-standing business partnership with a disrespectful and insulting partner. Do you

(A) deny and repress your hurt feelings to keep the peace or

(B) refuse to tolerate anything less than a respectful and professional relationship?

5. You've held the same job for several years and find it unfulfilling, but you feel called to be more. Do you

(A) keep your nose to the grindstone at work, hoping for a promotion or

(B) start taking online courses and doing research about entrepreneurship?

6. A family member who has criticized your artistic ability discovers you're interested in turning your passion for art into a business. Do you

(A) let them talk you out of moving forward or

(B) ignore their negativity and pursue your business anyway?

7. Your small business isn't so small anymore. Your income now surpasses anything you've ever earned from a traditional job. But people in your community are accusing you of being a snob because you can afford more than they can. Do you

(A) feel embarrassed and guilty for being so successful or

(B) continue to work toward your goals, grateful for the opportunity to support your family and give to charity?

8. You find out about a business mentorship in your field that is only slightly out of budget for you. Do you

(A) delay getting mentoring for your business until you have all your ducks in a row or

(B) find creative ways to afford the mentorship like selling some belongings in order to start learning as soon as possible?

Insights:

- **If you did not answer (A) at all,** you live your life with a faithful heart, confident in God's love and abiding support. That faith allows you to thrive joyfully outside your comfort zone. You understand that God works through you to encourage and lead others to push the self-imposed limits of their own comfort zones.

- **If you answered (A) only once or twice,** you don't allow fear to control your life. You believe that Papa has your back, and you generally feel strong in your faith. At times, the criticism of others or your own inner critic can get the best of you, but you tend not to let that hold you back.

- **If you responded with roughly half (A's) and half (B's)** you may feel unsteady in your faith, and therefore in your life. The voice of your inner critic can be loud, clamping down your true potential. If it wasn't for your faith, you wouldn't challenge yourself to take on new experiences. But you feel called to be more than who you are now, so you try and face your fears.

- **If you answered (A) at least six times,** then your fear may be overcoming your faith. You believe in God, yet fear has a grasp on your spirit, and it's holding you back from achieving your true potential—and from being the person Papa God has created you to be.

- **If you responded (A) every time,** you may be listening to the voice of fear above all else, letting it drown out the steadfast and loving voice of Papa God. Consider spending more time developing a relationship with your loving Father, knowing that He has great plans for you.

Your answers to this simple yet powerful quiz can reveal whether fear or faith wields the most power in your life. Embracing the beautiful and loving voice of Papa brings unlimited possibilities to your life. It will drown out the destructive voice of fear that is holding you back from achieving your full potential and living your purpose.

Grab a Journal!

We get more of what we focus on. Where has your focus been lately? On the worst-case scenario or option? Fear or faith? If we multiply that which we give most of our attention to, what are you producing in your life? What do you WANT to produce in your life?

RESISTANCE: WE WEREN'T BORN AFRAID

If I could take you back to the day when you took your first steps, and let you hear the thoughts that were in your mind that day, you know what you wouldn't hear? Well, I do. I can guarantee you wouldn't hear the voice of unworthiness. No one-year-old is thinking, "Who am I to get up on my feet and make a move for that cookie? Who do I think I am to imagine I'm good enough to have a cookie in the first place?" No. She's just thinking "cookie."

And figuring out how to get to that treat in the best way possible. And when she falls down, as she inevitably will—dozens of times—she will just get back up and try again. She is learning. And missteps are simply part of learning. Judgment has no place there. But, sadly, it isn't long before judgment arrives, creating the path for resistance to show up too.

We aren't born hearing the voice of unworthiness. It comes from family members who let us know we've disappointed them. It comes from teachers who tell us we don't measure up as they hand us the paper with the F. Or the A-. Both can be failure depending on what you believe. And pretty soon, we don't need those external voices doubting us. We've created a script in our own heads. Even as children. Just a few years after we've taken those first brave steps, resistance shows up as judgment and fear.

And the voice of fear spreads the false message that you are not enough, and that you never will be. We grow up listening to this voice. It is the voice of lack, and the voice of emotional, spiritual, and financial poverty. Know that everyone hears this voice, but no one has to listen to it. I feel you can choose to tune it out and instead be filled with the love of Papa God, and to hear the message that you are not only worthy—but that you are limitless in what you can achieve in your life.

Spiritual Takeaway

Who am I? I am someone uniquely created by Papa God to make a difference in the world.
When I increase in wealth and reach my potential as a human being, I can become a life changer for myself and for others!

CHAPTER 8

BUSINESS AS UN-USUAL

When I lived in Indiana for four years, the Amish in the area had several stores that I loved to visit. One time a shop owner showed me how they roasted their coffee beans, taking extra care as each fragrant bag was packaged, carefully sealing it with love by getting all the trapped air out of the bag. He looked at me and smiled. "I want you to experience a cup of coffee just as I do with every single pot you make. It's an experience that should never be rushed through and will not soon be forgotten." My heart was struck by how sincere he was and how he treated me like family. I felt like the only person that mattered in that moment.

I loved visiting Amish shops like this one. Not because I wanted their lifestyle, but because the warm, inviting atmosphere of the coffee shop, the kid's store, the specialty blanket shop, and the consignment shop made me feel like I was "home" in a sense. I was in a place that was safe, inviting, and even comforting. My guard didn't go up, because no one was trying to sell me or push me into buying anything. They sincerely loved being able to serve people, and were making a good living out of it. Five generations had lived their lives, fed their families, and built their dreams in this community. Their prices were fair, they served with love, and on top of that, they were making a profit. Business as usual was not so "usual" within this community of people. But it was working. Their bottom line wasn't money. It was love. This inspired me to create core values in my own company that would make my customers, and even my employees, feel loved and valued in the same way.

The Amish people seemed to wear their hearts on their sleeves, in a good sort of way. They shared the personal sides of their lives with me, and I never felt that they were trying to take advantage of me or any of their customers. They didn't seem to have an agenda, other than to serve with love.

THE POWER OF LOVE

Loving your customers is about *service*, not sales. Like most people, I hate to be sold to, but if you *serve* me better than the shop down the street does, I'm coming back to see you again and again. I'll even pay more for the same product because you make me feel valued. Loved, even.

Yes, loved. That's how I want my customers to feel. I know, that's not business as usual. In fact, bringing love into commerce is an unusual way of doing business. Too many business owners have been programmed to believe that we shouldn't get too close, or get personally involved with our customers, or things will start to deteriorate. I mean, it's all about getting the sale, right? Maybe that's what they teach in business school. I don't know. College wasn't my path. So I never learned the expected steps or guidelines to make a sale. So I'm not guided (or limited) by any business doctrine. Instead I'm led by my heart. And the remarkable thing is that caring for people as I'd want to be cared for has always proven to bring results, both in my life and in my businesses. This is one of the secrets to my success. By creating an environment built on relationships with people, they genuinely trust you. And you care about them, so you want the very best for them. So everything you create is about helping them succeed. Which in turn creates incredible success for you, the business owner, because people buy from businesses they trust. The foundation of my business is the fact that my customers mean the world to me. It's an honor to serve them. Love is a natural outworking of that service.

LOVE IN ACTION

Want your customers to start loving you? And to show love back to them? Smile when you're on the phone. Ask your clients what they want. If someone wants their money back, return it cheerfully. And go the extra mile. Take the time to give people what they really paid for. You know, most people who ask for a refund really don't want one. Does that surprise you? They just feel as if their original buy-in is no longer there. So go back to that. How can YOU take some extra time to help THEM get what they originally wanted with their purchase? Take customer loyalty seriously. Build community with your clients.

One of the biggest paybacks of loving your customers is how it affects your team as a whole, your company mission, and how it sets you apart in a marketplace where far too many companies are just focusing on closing the sale and not on the happiness of the consumer. Loving your customers changes the dynamic. It makes all the difference in the world.

The *business as un-usual* things that I've created came out of a flow of my own personal freedom. Having the courage to ask Papa God for what I want in life and in work, and doing things that deviate completely from business as usual, have proven to not only be hugely successful for me, but it also inspires others to do things in their unique way, and we all win.

One of the things I do is to bring faith into the workplace, not in a way that alienates anyone, but in a much more powerful way in which people of different faiths are respected and honored.

FAITH AT WORK

The concepts of loving people and bringing our faith to work are not just for people who call themselves Christians. Yes, anyone can tell from my websites, videos, and quote graphics that

I'm a radical, out-of-the-box Jesus lover. He's my DNA. You can't talk to me for very long without realizing that Papa and I are more than just friends, we are co-creators together, in business and in life. We're always talking, interacting, seeing, inspiring, and reaching for more. During my workday you may even hear me say a few expletives to resistance and the enemy. I may notice that opposition has entered the room, and it's not in people. I might also ask Holy Spirit to come and do what we can't do— solve a problem, settle a matter with a disgruntled customer who just can't seem to find any peace, give a co-worker grace through a difficult day, and even make our Facebook ads go to places that we never even paid for! Yeah, that's pretty radical, isn't it? My company has done over $2 million in Facebook ads in the last three years. But I know that our ads went to audiences we didn't target or pay for, and our content ended up in front of people because angels were on assignment doing more than we ever could have imagined doing on our own. That's a slight edge you don't typically hear about in the latest business meeting! Yet, it's a normal business day for us. Faith changes everything.

Don't think for one minute, though, that my client base is just filled with people who believe like I do. No way! This radical way of living and doing *business as un-usual* has attracted people of every background, faith, and belief. That's refreshing and exhilarating to me! I thrive in situations of diversity. I don't want to be surrounded by people who only think and believe as I do. That creates limits. I have an open mind *and* an open heart. Heck, my first choice for a date is someone of a different color! Papa wired me to be drawn to people who are unique and intriguing, even those who might be my polar opposite!

THE POWER OF LOVE IN BUSINESS

A big portion of the client base at my company believes differently than I do, but they find the truth in what I am saying and join me in a beautiful diverse harmony that brings unity like nothing I've ever seen in a local church. This is why faith belongs at work! When I see heaven move, and demons flee, it shows me the hand of Papa God in a way that most pastors have hoped for, but never quite had the courage to step out into. It's not a matter of laying aside our beliefs and saying they're no longer important. And it's not just about being tolerant of those who are different than we are. It's deeper than that. Much deeper.

Let me ask you this: Why should I be offended if my Muslim co-worker wants to pray at work? Does his free-will choice of believing in something different than I do mean that I should feel threatened, invalidated, or in some way unsafe? Just because he believes and practices his beliefs differently than I do, does this mean that I can't believe and live my Christian faith out alongside him at work, and accomplish great things in our company? No. It doesn't. We're not gathered at work as a place of worship; we're there to bring value to the marketplace, to serve the world, and to bring a product or service to the public. In this space, if we are able to fully be ourselves, and live in our own energy, beliefs, and faith together—well, imagine the power in that. Even as I write this, tears are rolling down my face and I just had my breath taken away. What if we stop trying to sectarianize ourselves into all being the same, or separating ourselves into all being disconnected? What if instead we open our hearts and minds to a harmony that is so powerful in the workplace, that we accomplish great things together, and transform cultures like no other generation that has gone before us?

Can I say it? Please? The most pathetic thing I've seen is when Christian business owners try to make all their staff like they are. It becomes a *Stepford Wives* sort of conformity. "You must be like this, believe like this, act like this, and check yourself out basically, and become a robot to work with us. Oh, and praise the Lord, bless God. He is good!" UGH. This is what has caused millions of people to hide their faith, pull away from each other, and disconnect their heart, and it has sadly turned the workplace into a place where we have to be on guard, self-protected, and not personally involved with anyone. It's created cliques and cultlike separation in the midst of all of us, and has taken us to a place where we're not even thinking straight anymore. If we all worked together to embrace each other, love, and accept each other, and we made it our mission to help one another REMEMBER who we are, the great world we would create would change swiftly. Our hearts would be realigned to the things that matter, and the first things first would stay first. Love, loyalty, trust, and openness would become the new norm in the marketplace. If each of us is at peace in our own soul because we are free to be who we really are when we come to work, we could quite possibly collide with all that Papa God intended for us, every single day.

Many people who believe as I do subscribe to a toxic view of the workplace, with a domination and dominion mind-set. I'm talking more about infiltration. If we want freedom in the workplace, it cannot and should not be a "Christian only" thing. Let's focus more on making a difference, and on changing cities and cultures through our lives and our work. If people come to know who they are, feel the love of Papa God, or even *just have a better day*, we've all won!

It's in our ordinary day-to-day lives where we really need to start seeing miracles. So many run to a church, or a meeting, or a movement to encounter the love of Papa God and a changed life. But what if we love people, and let Papa God get back into the business of saving them? I'm in the business I am in because I love it, it's an outworking of who I am, and it gives me an added quality of life. I'm not trying to save people. That's not my job. My job is to LOVE. Papa is in the business of saving.

GET OVER IT

What if we added humility, honor, and forgiveness to our business plans, and actually took the golden rule seriously? It's time to get over our stereotypes and judgments about other religions when we're at work. I mean it. GET OVER IT. Yes, there are bad examples. But the truth of the matter is it's ridiculous to think that every Muslim is a terrorist or every Christian is a nutcase trying to beat someone into submission with a black leatherette Bible. Yes, many people use religion as a scapegoat, a way to get power, and as an escape. Sure there are bad examples. But there are also plenty of people who embrace their faith and are letting love win in their lives daily. Sadly, many of them are also hiding out in the workplace and aren't letting their faith become evident. What if a new level of honor, a culture of honor if you will, became our focus, rather than tolerance?

Let's stop defending what we believe, or subscribe to, by using extreme examples to prove our point so everyone will listen. People are sick of the extreme examples that don't do anything to change how they feel at work. Love can exist in a culture that is honorable, and when we inspire people to know WHO they are, what they do at work will change. Creativity will increase, strategy will come together, and innovations we've needed for centuries will be released!

It gives me courage and empowers me to be with people who are of a diverse spiritual background in my workplace. This causes me to think differently and consider possibilities, and opens my mind to options I've never seen before in my locked-away, hiding-behind-the-computer existence. Seeing people step into their full power and abilities is my fuel! It also gives me courage to do things my way in my companies. I see this as a movement, and it only takes one person to pioneer a movement that can change the world. Anomaly behavior became my normal MO when things never made sense.

And by the way, it was never my intention to create a little church in the marketplace. My experiences with church were not good, so why the heck would I want to bring that into my company? Ironically, when I was first on social media, a lot of people thought they had the right to regulate, admonish, and, quite frankly, take authority over me and the way I did things simply because I identified myself as a Christian. This made me disgusted! The religious spirit was everywhere. But I channeled all that negative energy and judgment to a place of inspiration and creativity with Papa. This caused me to go outside the artificial boundaries and boxes of typical commerce and pioneer things way before their time.

AHEAD OF MY TIME

For example, in the late 1990s, it was not common for online businesses to have free shipping. People were concerned with how the Internet was being used, and were closely monitoring and protecting their brick-and-mortar investments. But when they came online, they were like tightwads gone astray, complaining about this expense and that cost, as if everything should be free online. Where did this mind-set come from? Is it because it's so convenient and easy to work online that we now think it should be free? I don't know, but I tapped into that feeling of wanting something to be free in my online business—high-end kitchenware—by giving free shipping on any order over $100. A few bumps in the road almost got in my way, like forgetting to limit this to the continental USA. Yeah. Shipping something for free to another country could cost me three times what the product itself was valued at. So I made many mistakes along the way. That's what a pioneer does. Then the opportunity arises to teach other aspiring online businesspeople how to avoid these pitfalls. That's what I do today in my Inner Circle academy for small business owners.

Back then, other online business owners in similar industries thought I was completely out of my mind for offering free shipping. They couldn't figure out how I was making money with such a tactic. But I couldn't figure out why other small business owners couldn't do the math. Their problem was not the free shipping. Their problem was in getting enough customers, period. If you're only doing five sales per week, yes, free shipping could kill your bottom line. But if you're doing five sales per hour, six days per week, the free shipping strategy can give you a great write-off at the end of the year, attract more customers, and become the deciding factor for where people will shop. Some people will even buy things they don't need just because it's attached to a free shipping offer! True story. Buyer's remorse, hesitation, and "I need to think about it" were eliminated with free shipping. It was and still is crucial in selling physical products that must be shipped. It's also so common today that many people won't even look at an online store that doesn't offer free shipping! Heck, Amazon now offers free shipping on the same day, for crying out loud. We've come a long way, baby! While I'm definitely not responsible for this current trend, it is very obvious to me that we tapped into something way ahead of its time.

FAITH IN ACTION

Another anomaly habit we used was taking a minute to pray over our ads, pray over our web pages, inviting heaven in, and getting into agreement. But this doesn't just happen behind closed doors and computer screens in my small home office. No, I've been known to pray over ads that I was writing for multi-billion-dollar companies. One particular client comes to mind. They trusted me to help them increase their online sales and to mirror what they were doing offline on their social media platform. They were a 2-billion-dollar corporation. I remember being on a live video chat with their marketing team, and feeling like things weren't connecting as well as I had hoped. So I took a minute to pray. Yup. I did it. But not in the way that most people might think. This was not a moment when I was greater than they were, telling them that we had to ask Papa for His approval of our work. Not at all. It was my way of saying that if they only got "professional me" when I did work for them, we'd all be sorely disappointed. So I went on to explain that I'm used to working with angels and helpers, and I wanted all the help I could get for their project.

So I took a minute, shut my eyes, and said, "Papa God, we need to get into agreement with heaven. Come and do what I can't do on my own, through me, for this client. They deserve the best, and I want them to do better than they've ever done before. So I'm asking for wisdom, grace, insight, quick recall, and strategy that is straight from heaven right now. Amen."

I heard a few sighs in the virtual conference room. It was almost as if something broke free. Someone muttered, "Wow, that was cool." Another person commented, "That was not what I expected at all." I opened my eyes with a big smile and said, "Okay, now! Let's get to work!" and everyone was thrilled. We had great results with that campaign and many of the other campaigns I had the honor to do with them. But the greatest thing that happened is that an infectious desire to serve the customer well, bring joy to the meetings, and simply enjoy each other while we worked together infiltrated the project. It was amazing. This may never have happened if I didn't have courage to just be myself and to work like I always do, even with people who might not get me, like me, or celebrate me.

I DON'T NEED YOU TO GET ME

Could it be that because I didn't need them to understand me, they actually began to? I had enough confidence to be fully myself even though I was in a business setting. To me, being my true, authentic self means I don't separate who I am personally and professionally. I am the same person wherever I am. A faith-based person. That's where my confidence comes from.

And to me, confidence is a self-assurance that comes from believing in your worth and abilities. Believing in who YOU are made to be and WHO you are not only gives confidence, but it is a gift back to heaven for all that you've been given. When we don't need someone to understand us in order to be whole, we actually draw people to us who will ultimately really "get" us. Bring this confidence into the workplace and you'll see swift changes. I'm not praying over my ads because I'm better than you, I need you to see how different we are, or because for some reason I need your approval and acceptance. No. I'm doing this because I know what happens when I do. I understand clearly who I am. I know my own capacity, and in the quietness of my office, I know I have encountered the God who is there, cares, and wants to be involved in every aspect of my life and career. That is what I want over the work I do for you, honestly. It's my gift to you—giving you my truest and best self. I'm already whole, powerful, and wise. I bring that to our business relationship. Imagine if everyone got to this place of strength and courage at work? We'd see radical changes.

WHAT DO YOU REALLY WANT?

You see, most of my life I had been told to lay aside my desires, to just be happy with what I had, and to find peace in not asking for anything. Just be content. Don't make waves. Stop being so selfish. Who cares what you want? These were constant messages that were instilled in me. It got to the point where I honestly had no clue what I wanted.

What do I want? To be loved. To be pursued with love. To feel safe and without panic all the time. Then my heart went into other desires. A fast car. To live in the mountains. To be pain free. Have more energy. Get back to the gym and never leave that lifestyle again. Get my body back. Regain the physical strength that I knew many years ago! To end autoimmune disease in my body. To be able to stop taking prescription pain medication. To be understood. To help businesses in Africa. To take three vacations a year that are each at least two weeks long. To meet a man who will see my journey and adore me and all my imperfections, who will pursue me, treat me like a queen, and desire me. My list of wants came forth from the depths of my heart. As I write this, I'm realizing that every single one of these desires has happened. Wow. Just WOW.

BIG-PICTURE LESSON

When is the last time you gave yourself permission to say or write out the things you want? It could be that the very things you thought were silly that are actually key to the divine purpose God has designed for your life and career. Maybe, just maybe, that thing that gets you into trouble, that wildness, or the ability to stay reserved under pressure that drives people crazy is actually something He is trying to do and use. Ignore the judgments and critics! Many times the criticism is confirmation that you're doing something great. It's proof of being in the midst of things that have purpose.

What do you want? Allow yourself the space to really write it out. What is the difference between want and desire for you? Do you have a hard time differentiating between desire and deserve? When we get to the place where we can be very clear on what we want, we'll get very clear on what we'll receive.

Some of you are called to lead, and some of you are called to help. Not all of us will have the opportunity or desire to start our own business. Each of us is beautifully and amazingly unique, and that will show up in its truest way when you embrace what you're made for. Your gifts, talents, and abilities are full of God's infinite wisdom, and were knit into your DNA at this time period, in this season, for such a time as this. What if you ask Papa to open up your eyes, make your ears more sensitive to His voice, and really take the time to start acting on the things you're seeing and hearing?

Let your mind go there for a few minutes.

What if you did all that you were created for?

What if we all did this and we collectively saw the power in all of it?

We could transform the world around us and create a new way of being and doing life for every one of us.

Let's invent the possibility that if we all did what we were created for, we could collectively and quickly transform nations and create a new way of doing life for every single one of us. And stop being so afraid of money, for crying out loud! Some of you are more afraid of money than you are the devil, and you've changed the bright, brilliant, supernatural aspects of God into a theological tenant that is predicable, clinical, and philosophical. As long as you can explain and control it all, you feel safe. No. This isn't safety, it's bondage, and it's ruining our lives!

Rising up into your purpose and calling isn't about being rebellious and destructive. It's not about raising flags and carrying protesting signs on every issue under the sun. Rather, it's a silent determination to remember who we are, individually, and then come together in acceptance and love, collectively.

And when you bring love into everything you do, not just in life, but in a very intentional way in business, you will see extraordinary results. Business as un-usual can be the most successful path for anyone who thinks beyond the traditional model of profit first and instead embraces service first.

ANOMALY ACTION: VALUE PEOPLE BEFORE PROFIT

People will go where they feel they are best being served. I've never forgotten that lesson, learned from kind and loving Amish shopkeepers years ago. Because of their beliefs, the Amish don't look to technology. Instead, their businesses grow on a foundation of simple values that truly resonate with their customers and can be embraced by anomalies in business everywhere. Utilize these ideas as Anomaly Actions to grow your business:

1. **Never try to sell something you don't truly believe in.** Your name is valuable and what you do in business is going to be directly attached to your name. Because of this high standard of integrity, don't market or sell anything you don't believe in. Regardless of the money, the demand in the marketplace, or the opinions of others, lead your company with integrity.

2. **Care deeply about your customers as people.** The Amish don't just serve their customers. They love them. The local coffee shop in a small town I used to go to served some of the best coffee I've ever had in my life. But truth be told, it's not the coffee beans that made it taste so amazing. It was the environment. An Amish family gutted out and redid an old building in a small, quaint town. They became one of the most profitable and successful businesses in the entire town. Caring for people with genuine hospitality is a big key to their success.

3. Think and act differently than everyone else and people will honor you for it. The Amish imbue their faith into every aspect of their lives. Because of this, when they serve you, care for you, price their products, market themselves, etcetera, they do it differently as well. During a recession I saw an Amish man expand his coffee business when he purchased a local warehouse in the same town. He now has a drive-thru-only coffee shop that serves passersby on their way to work or just for the day! Think about it. Though it isn't part of his own life to own a car, he knows his customers do. So he makes sure to serve his customers who drive. Different, isn't it?

4. Stay connected to your customers and clients. This is an old-fashioned business principal that so many companies neglect. Even with the ease of e-mail and the simplicity of social media and blogging, far too many businesses simply do not "touch" their clients enough in any given month. It's no small wonder their promotions and sales don't work! The Amish don't view you as simply a customer; they see you as someone to serve.

5. Work when everyone else is asleep. When most people are sleeping in on a Saturday morning, many Amish families have already been awake for hours. Milking cows, rolling bread dough, getting the oven hot for today's baking—it all happens way before the sun rises. They rise while it is still night and work diligently with their hands. They serve others at the first part of the day and are many times given "brand loyalty" because of this one thing. Does this mean that you have to work 90 hours per week to be successful? Not at all, but if you take this tip from the Amish, and you work hard when most people are sleeping on their dreams and are giving in to drama and emotions, you too will prosper when others struggle.

> ## Grab a Journal!
>
> Do you have any blocks in your spirit or soul about doing business with any specific "type" of people? List out any judgments, blocks, or triggers that come up. Do you find yourself only drawn to working with men? Or working with only women? Why? It might be because of the type of product or business you represent, but it could be because of judgments and blocks. This is where we want to go. When we value people more than profit, the profit will grow as we learn to love people more.

RESISTANCE: YOUR METRON

You may feel pressured to do things the "expected way." To be a success in a way that doesn't feel successful to you at all. You are now experiencing outward resistance. So much of resistance is within. You know, how we tell ourselves we're different—like that's a bad thing—and that we don't fit in. We feel inner pressure to conform. That kind of resistance is what I've been talking about in previous chapters. But outward resistance is pressure from family, friends, and society, telling you to act like everyone else. If you allow this pressure to change the path that feels right to you—your unique purpose—you won't be at peace in your life or in your work.

The Bible teaches that we have a God-given divine sphere of influence. We have a measure, a marked-off ability, that can give us safety, security, and enormous capacity! It's called a Metron, which is our measure, and within this measure is everything we need to be successful in the career paths we choose—if we choose from our hearts. That doesn't mean it will always be easy, or will happen no matter what. But it does mean that you'll have divine connection and enablement in this realm that can fuel you forward when everything seems like it's against you. It's a place of ease. Resistance loses power over you when you embrace your Metron. It's your positioning in life.

You're not just a seed seeking to be planted so that you can bear much fruit. You're a forest! Inside your measured capacity and influence are worlds yet unknown and adventures drawing us in! Remember my trip to heaven? Imagine that you have a design and creative room in heaven attached to your personal Metron. Now would you believe Papa God and get into agreement? If so, business and life as un-usual can become your new norm.

God's love and power are measureless! You'll be shocked at how far you can go in your divine enablement. There are no limits!

The truth is, you and I aren't like everyone else. We are anomalies. We learn differently. We feel differently. We succeed differently. So hold tight to your true self regardless of the pressure you feel to be like everyone else. Being yourself is the ultimate success.

Spiritual Takeaway

I can love people in business and life without losing who I am. My service is shown through love, and is valued because I love. I attract amazing clients into my life whom I have the honor to love through my business and my life.

CHAPTER 9

THE ANOMALY EFFECT

I remember the one-bedroom apartment in Michigan that I shared with my son when he was just a baby. I was just 24 years old. Wow. Even as I write that out, it seems like such a very long time ago, and in other places of my heart, it seems like just yesterday. Thirty years ago, I wasn't running a big business, interacting with people all over the world, and helping others. No, I was a single mommy trying to figure out how to help myself.

I can still see the couch that had a huge hole in it because the previous owner's Great Dane had apparently needed a snack! Covering the hole with a handed-down blanket made it perfect. It was a 400-square-foot apartment, and I was raising my son by myself there. We didn't have any extras or nice things, but we had what we needed, and, most importantly, we had each other. His crib sat just two feet from my twin mattress that was laid out on the floor. It was ours. It was home. Building my first business as a single mommy raising my young prince alone, my focus was simply to make enough money to get out of the poverty we were living in.

I had no clue I'd make a million dollars six years later. No clue at all.

At that time in 1990 our income was $5,000 per year from my cleaning jobs. The way I made ends meet and provided what we needed was through governmental supplementation and a LOT of prayer. It was in these early years as a single mommy that I really found the heart of God, and I discovered that I could move mountains with mustard seed–sized faith.

FINDING A WAY

Because I didn't want my son to be raised by someone else, or in a day care setting, it didn't occur to me to look at job boards, find a career counselor, or figure out how to go back to school to create a new future for the two of us. Instead, I just began to brainstorm the sorts of "jobs" that I could do on my own. I went to the library to do some research. That led me to a possibility that I could transform something I already loved to do into my chosen profession. I could create a path out of struggle and suffering. The answer was cleaning. I loved it. It was rewarding to me, and something I never grew tired of. I studied how to clean all sorts of surfaces. You name it. Linoleum, asphalt, ceramic, wood, and more. Smiley's Cleaning Service was born!

My wish to be the mommy I was meant to be, taking care of my son while he was little, and giving him my time and my heart, came true through a broom, a mop, and a vacuum.

It was a very scary thing to go against the traditional path of getting a college degree, finding a job, and living happily ever after. Finding my own work, creating my own job, and doing things on my own was not something anyone ever talked to me about. As I look back to that time in my life, it startles me to think that I had no personal examples of anyone working for themselves, but my courage was so big in this area of my life, that I didn't care or even feel a need for that.

The name Smiley's Cleaning Service came to me because people always said my smile could light up the world. Being an optimistic, happy, and energetic person was my normal way of being, despite the fact that I had endured such a painful life. Pushing all my feelings and triggers aside, I became a "business owner" in my head. You see, playing a role was never a challenge for me. I was like a professional actress who could become anything she had to be. Whenever I was in a situation that I wasn't familiar with, my focus became to find someone I could follow so I could study what they did. The concept of modeling—watching what someone else does and patterning yourself after them in your own unique way—was unknown to me, but that is exactly what I did. Finding books about small business and researching articles in magazines about people who were doing it became my first "training academy" in my classroom of self-taught business. As I read that people would name their companies something that helped their customers identify who they were, Smiley became the first thing that jumped into my mind.

I headed to a local office supply store and got my very first set of business cards printed. I remember using the money from my very first cleaning job to get those business cards, as well as my cleaning supplies, and anything else I needed. My first job came as a referral from my sister to her friend. The first house I ever cleaned was more than 4,800 square feet in the wealthiest neighborhood I had ever seen. Debbie hired me on the spot when I came to meet her in person and give her a quote. As I explained that she'd be my first client, and it would help me to know what she's accustomed to paying for her house cleaning, we negotiated a price and I was on my way! Thirty years later and I live in a 5,400-square-foot home on the side of a mountain, and have an amazing cleaning lady that I helped negotiate my price with. Isn't life amazing? We never know where our humble beginnings will take us.

Debbie let me use her cleaning supplies, and I soon discovered most people I cleaned for would also be this way. They had their favorites, and the kind of vacuum that they wanted used. So I didn't have to come up with much to be in business! A few more referrals and an ad in the local *Macomb Daily* newspaper and I had a full schedule cleaning homes, and enough money coming in to change my son's and my life forever.

It wasn't just our financial future that was changed, however. My son would go with me while he was little and sit in his little baby carrier. As he got older he stayed in his playpen, and I'd clean with him right there with me. When another year went by and he became three years old, I knew I would have to find something else to do. Knowing this full well going into it, I wasn't bothered. Because I knew that Papa would always make a way for me. My faith was so strong at this time in my life, despite my income being very small, and my apartment being even smaller.

The more housecleaning clients I got, the more my exposure to a bigger life opened up. Many of the people I cleaned for owned their own companies and had really big homes with decorations and furniture like I'd never seen before. Eventually I got calls from doctors and lawyers in Grosse Pointe, the area known for millionaires and the well-off, and my exposure to bigger business, a bigger life, and more money grew. Initially I felt so out of place around these people, like the poor single mom who needed a handout rather than the businesswoman I had become. I believe many of my clients picked up on this and began to speak life over me. As I think back, they used to compliment me like crazy for my work ethic, how focused I was, and how committed I was to being on time, getting things done efficiently, and creating a schedule for their home that both of us loved. However, my mind was so full of pain, and so used to being knocked down, that although my company began to grow, my heart and opinion of myself wouldn't feel it for a long time.

HITTING A CROSSROAD

As I began to clean more houses, and the houses grew in size and, naturally, the length of time it took for me to clean them, I hit a big problem. One that can often happen with small business owners. It was my first experience with having so much work I personally could not do it all. So I went back to the library to see what others were doing. Thumbing my way through the yellow pages, phone call after phone call was made, listening to how professional cleaning companies and other small businesses who were doing what I did answered their phone lines. My dream of hiring other people to work for me and clean houses with me grew. But the reality of lazy uncommitted employees, people who wanted an easy life not a career they could be proud of, grew as well. This was NOT working for me. So after firing three people in a month, my mind did what it always seems to do. I looked for a solution to my problem!

It became apparent that I should find the next level in the cleaning business world. Isn't that what all small business owners did? In the books I read they did, so this is what I pursued. But the only way to make more money cleaning homes was to clean more homes, or larger homes—both of which took more time. My ceiling was time and energy. My body began to hurt, and I was exhausted by the end of the week. Many times I got sick from pushing myself so hard. Depression began to set in, and I knew I didn't want my son living with a mommy sunk in despair, so I searched cleaning companies in the yellow pages. What I discovered opened up new possibilities for me—office cleaning. This was a whole new world! And it wasn't easy to get into. I answered ads, placed ads, went to big buildings and asked questions about who cleaned for them, and discovered that while the pay was nearly triple that of house cleaning, so were the requirements, commitment, amount of work, and experience.

THE SOLUTIONIST

Then I saw an ad for a hospital that was hiring a cleaning person to take over the Prompt Care Facilities. It was a full-time position, and they were paying an hourly wage that was way below what I was used to. The memory comes to me now that I didn't accept what they had created as the only solution.

I didn't have Facebook to help me gather opinions. Facebook wasn't even thought of yet, and being able to see how other people did things online hadn't even entered my mind. But I'm a solutionist, so I created a plan and went on my first interview with the intention of converting the interviewer's mind to what I saw. This skill set was first learned when I worked in my early 20s as a waitress, and later as a bartender who got the highest tips and made a ton of money listening to people, starting conversations, and leading people in the direction I wanted them to go. That skill came in handy when I met with the HR person at the hospital. As the conversation started in a traditional way for an interview, I began to answer her questions with questions about how flexible or open to new ideas they might be. She said they were always open to new things, as long as it didn't put the hospital and its patients at risk. Laying out my plan for working three nights per week, from 8 P.M. to 12 A.M., my concept of how to clean the Prompt Care Facilities was born, and so was my new career.

As I think back to this event, I'm shocked, really, that they gave me this job so quickly. Nowadays I'd have to be bonded, licensed, screened, drug tested, and more. But not then. Favor, God, and who the heck knows what else blew the door open for me! I used my best skills and the smile that everyone knew me for, and with one interview that led to meeting the head of the facilities, I was contracted to do two locations on the spot. They said it would be a trial run for 30 days, but I knew that I'd be the best they ever had. And I was. They said so over and over again.

So, I hired a college-aged girl to come babysit while I was gone cleaning, as my son slept at night. It was great! In 1991 I was making $320 to $400 per week. It took me three hours per night, and I had regular work. Each of the two facilities paid me $120 per week, and I got another office to clean along with my Prompt Care Facilities. I worked Monday through Friday at night and had all my days and weekends to be with my son, doing what I loved the most—being his mommy. As is the case with governmental assistance, I was on my own very quickly. WIC was no longer an option, so there were no more food stamps or help. This was the first time I realized I was on my own with taking care of my son, and it overwhelmed me. I had no one to model for this either. No one I could look up to who'd overcome insurmountable odds and came out shining. So while my career grew, and my mothering did as well, so did an enormous amount of shame and fear, coupled with daily worrying about how long I could do all of this, provide for my son, and live on my own without any help.

In my mind, I figured everyone who didn't want to leave their children, or who wanted more freedom, or didn't want to be strapped to a boss just created a job that they could do. It never even entered into my mind that everyone was *not* doing this, and that instead many people were just struggling, or complaining about their situation, and that some of them were doing nothing. It didn't make any sense to me when people said that the only reason this worked for me was because I was special, or even specially gifted. To me it was an easy equation—working for someone else does not equal the free time and kind of income I wanted. So I did something about it. But even with all my solutions, things that worked and changed in our lives, I was still a broken little girl (who was attacked as a young woman and then grew up to be a mommy), and my heart hurt daily.

THE STRUGGLE CONTINUES

Thinking differently was something I wrestled with for most of my life. I was thinking that I was broken, not right, or incomplete. The pain I had experienced in my life, all 26 years of it at this point, taught me to be a solutionist and a self-starter. But it didn't teach me how to handle not comparing myself with others, being my own person, and rising as an anomaly. The thing people attacked and misunderstood about me the most was the way I always did things against the grain, in the opposite direction of the tide, and in my own unique way. But I never saw this as the genius I was made to be. To me, it was a weakness and something to hide.

Let me interject here that some of you are also wired with a unique way to think about things, and you have a very different perspective when it comes to challenges, problems, and solutions. Unfortunately, you've been judged, told to get your heads out of the clouds, and have had your unique way of thinking squashed by a spirit of skepticism, fear, and control. My prayer for you is that this book stirs up something inside of you to shake that off so you can take back the unique way Papa God gave you to think. Look at it this way: how you think differently can hold answers for your life and many lives that will connect with you.

Maybe you joined millions of people who plan out their future and pursue their dreams by consulting with colleges and career counselors. "Get a degree, get a good job, and live happily ever after." Now this might work if you go to school to be a doctor, or a lawyer, or something else that absolutely necessitates that you get a degree. But no one ever talks about whether or not the job you chose is in high demand. No one pays attention to the huge price tag this promise comes with. There's no one to teach you how to market yourself, get out there, and get a job! It's almost like a Ponzi scheme because it makes it sound like education is the key to a great-paying career. No, it's not. *Doing something with your education is.* Making sure the education you get is something that is needed in the career you choose. Also, where are the teachers our young people really need? The ones helping them to identify their innate gifts, talents, and abilities, and activating these so that they can pursue the career of their dreams that they were *made for*?

It's often not until a year after graduation that disillusioned people with no jobs and a massive amount of debt realize that things aren't going to work out as planned. Far too many people with big degrees still struggle to make ends meet, and even worse, get a job where they don't even use their degree. While I'm not against college or getting an education, the reality is this: the marketplace pays for value. Whether this value comes from going to college, getting a degree, and getting extremely good at what you do, or by attending conferences, self-studying your way to mastery, and then getting specialized in good old-fashioned hard work—the service or product that people pay for has to add value on their end.

So, I believe that *freedom* should be our pursuit, not a college degree and letters after our name.

A BIG LIFE

Initially the only goal I had was to one day spend enough time with my son so that he didn't have to be raised by someone else. It was through my cleaning business that I first met my now ex-husband. It was through my cleaning company that I was spurred on to keep dreaming about a better life. And my life continued on. Then after I got married and had two more sons, I left my cleaning career behind to finally be "taken care of" by the man I had married. But I'd soon realize that the exposure I had to millionaires, bigger homes, and bigger lives would come back to me as I dreamed of a big life for my family. So, when my ex-husband's income couldn't provide the high-end kitchenware I wanted in my home, I did what was always the answer for me—I took things into my own hands and made a way! I started the online kitchenware business using the same skills I'd learned with Smiley's Cleaning Service.

As I shared earlier, my very first online business was in selling high-end kitchenware like blenders, kitchen mixers, grain mills, and coffee makers. Eventually I had over 400 items we'd drop ship. All I ever wanted was the best tools and machines in my own kitchen so I could have a great experience preparing meals and bread for my family. I wanted us to be able to go out to dinner anytime we wanted to, or to pay cash for a vacation. I would later start a copywriting firm because I got really good at writing all my own marketing pages for my kitchen store, and then my vitamin stores.

My goals began to grow when I began to travel a bit, because I wanted to be able to "plug in" anywhere I was, working virtually wherever I chose, serving people all over the world. Step-by-step, my vision grew, my skill set and specialization grew, and so did my value. My company, A Real Change, was planned and created to help other small business owners do extraordinary things in their own businesses with very simple tools and strategies. My vision was to employ our entire family and to be able to work anywhere we wanted to. All three of my sons were launched into their future lives through that company! Freedom was always the goal, not business.

My heart and mind were craving freedom and creating the means to get there! I wanted freedom to live together, grow together, and impact people's lives, as a family. As our influence began to grow, so did the focus of who we could help! As our skill set increased, so did our focus on how much we could do for others. While I do love a challenge, and wanted to make more money so we could do anything we wanted to do, whenever we wanted to do it, the focus was not purely on money. But the money always followed my vision and focus. We never lacked one good thing. Every year we made gains, and every year more was given to us to steward.

MAKE IT WORK

If you were to map out a way to create freedom in your life, what does it look like? Are you immediately interrupted with thoughts of not being able to afford it? Switch to an anomaly mind-set! How can you make money or recycle what you have? When I didn't have $100 to do any ads, I began to sell online—10 items for $10. I didn't pray and fast and beg Papa to send me $100! No! I didn't try to come up with something that people could buy from me for $100! I simply took the lowest amount and multiplied it. Selling 10 items for $10 from my closet was easy. I sold things I loved—things I had bought on credit, and probably should have never purchased. I got rid of a lot. And as the money came back in, I bought better things. But I'll never forget the year when my entire wardrobe was purchased at a Goodwill store. I was selling all my clothes, and recycling them into ads for my company. The used consignment items I purchased were fine. I had no debt, my business was growing, and more importantly, I was happy! When we take the time to deviate from whatever is considered to be the norm, it's remarkable what we might come up with.

The "orphan mind-set" that I'd had of being alone, struggling, and not needing anyone, because people aren't safe, evolved. It grew into this "think on your own" businesswoman who could create things out of thin air and make enormous amounts of money. It's incredible to me that this came from pain and trauma. If you were to examine the obstacles and challenges you may have lived through, I wonder if it could lead to your strength. God is like that—He'll take our broken pieces and put them back together into something beautiful. That which the enemy thought would destroy, ruin, and break us forever becomes our slight edge in life. I love that!

BRANDING AND STANDING OUT IN BUSINESS

Conventional wisdom is rarely wise, and often limiting. To someone with an anomaly mind-set, unconventional thinking just comes naturally. One reason I created things new, on my own, is because the way that things were typically done just didn't make any sense to me. Now listen, that has been the case in A LOT of things that I've been hugely successful in! I remember an interview with a major publication that I had to do, and I was terrified. Seriously. They sought me out because of the results I created on social media, and here I was, completely baffled by their preliminary questions. None of it made any sense to me. As I read what they intended to ask me over the air, and later print on their website and in their magazine, I was filled with unusual fear. If it wasn't for my oldest son, who by this time was 28, interpreting what they were asking, I probably would have turned the entire thing down. Where I thought they were out in left field, they were simply describing things in a different way— in a way that typically confused me. This kind of thing happened to me often. You see, I got really good at things on my computer on my own, figuring it out, and calling it whatever I wanted to. But when I had to step up to the plate and "play with the big guys," not only did their uniforms not fit me, but I had no clue what language they were talking! It was very intimidating. Didn't make sense to me. But when I got the gist of what they meant, I created something new in my head so that I could relate.

Let me speak into that: some of you have felt like you're dumb, broken, or abnormal. Maybe teachers, parents, and those in authority have even gone so far as to say that the way you think isn't right or that you're somehow broken. If this is the case, I implore you to get some healing. You're not broken. You're an anomaly! Maybe others have to work hard to acquire and achieve certain things. But you, with a mind-set that deviates from most of that which is customary, well, you are *wired* for it. Your brain does it automatically, just like mine does!

This same thing happened when I was working on our branding. The whole concept of branding meant nothing to me, honestly. But as a successful business owner, and someone who had made millions of dollars selling things online for years, it was just expected that I would not only be able to talk about branding, but also be able to show everyone else how to brand themselves, their messages, and their businesses! All I could explain was my branding demonstrated my burning passion and the message I wanted to get across to my clients. It was what caused people to pay attention to and be attracted to me, and stop to listen to what I had to say on social media and through e-mail.

USING MY STRENGTHS

But I was never a polished, typical marketer who could stand in front of a white board and explain branding concepts, ROI strategies, or direct response statistics. I could, however, stand in front of the same white board and explain to you why people focus on a certain space on a web page, what to do to direct people to go elsewhere on your site, why certain words made people respond, and the patterns and trends that showed me why people ignore some messages. I would sit in my office, listening to worship music from Bethel Music and staring at 20 websites, and begin to see things illuminate and come into focus right in front of my eyes. When I thought about teaching big marketing firms this, it was scary. So I didn't. I simply taught them what I ended up learning in these hidden-away moments with heaven.

I was taught how to market, spot trends, and to see things in the spirit realm that would help my campaigns in the quietness of my early-morning meetings with Papa. God's love wasn't fractured or troubled. He would answer any question I ever asked of Him. When I wanted to learn how to write better sales copy, He never told me that wasn't allowed, or that He wasn't interested in such trivial matters.

No. He began to make things jump off the web pages, and He taught me over and over again. As I lay on the floor of my office, crying out for help, wisdom, strategy, and insight that the rest of the world didn't have, He, the God of the Universe, who knew every hair on my head, would answer me. Little ole me. The homemaker in Michigan who had a heart to believe He'd answer. I might not have had enough faith at that time in my life to have my heart healed of the trauma I had lived through, but I had enough faith to ask this all-powerful, all-knowing God how to grow my business.

Isn't it funny that my faith was so big for my business, but so small for my personal life? For many years, as I built my companies, religious people and the fraud police continued to infect the mind-set I had about myself. At least once a day I'd disqualify myself from motherhood, being a great wife, and knowing how to change my life and be a better woman; but when it came to asking God to teach me how to write Google or Facebook ads, my faith was huge.

BE FREE

Where are you today? Are there areas of your life where you feel like you can ask God anything? Does your faith soar unadulterated, unchanged? Are you like a child about some things, but when it comes to the real personal issues of life, do you still struggle? This, my friend, is where the closet doors of our lives must come open, and we must walk out. It's time for us to get real with ourselves, and real with others.

Some of you are so gifted and talented, and you've been judging yourself just as I had for many years. The comparison game started at a very young age for you as well. How many people have created boxes and borders to keep you out and spoken words to make you stay silent? You've heard their messages. Yet inside of you is this unlived life screaming to come out.

Let it.

My word for you is to stop trying to fit into things, systems, and methods of this life that God was never a part of and that He never created. Be free. Be who you are. Be your truest self. You deserve the pursuit of finding out who that is. The Lord *your* Peace is calling to you. It's time to be loving, kind, and honoring to *yourself,* so that you can be this toward others, even when they don't understand or get you. You'll never think like them, experience things as they do, and many times, you'll never be taken seriously because of these unique differences. But these things are your unique wiring and DNA. They are what you were created with and for.

Do your part to maintain your individuality. Do your part to create a diversity in harmony with others. We need to stop medicating our genius people and release the doors to these cages we've forced them to fit into. The genius people are our answers. *You,* my friends, might hold the keys to revolutionary breakthroughs in medicine, IT, business, social media, bitcoin, unknown galaxies, quantum physics, finance, and more. We need you, and if you try to fit into everyone's boxes, we'll never experience all that you were made for.

BIG-PICTURE LESSON

For as long as I can remember, a hypervigilance was inside of me—I was fighting to be free, fighting to stand up, dreaming and hoping to be applauded one day for being myself. But it never happened. Not until I began to share who I was, my heart, my constant thoughts, and my struggles on social media. And when it did happen, it wasn't praise or acceptance I was seeking, just simply someone who was like me, so we wouldn't be so isolated anymore. We didn't have to be alone ever again.

To be my unique self and understand the different seasons I've experienced has been the journey of my lifetime. Learning to not put old wine into new wineskins and also to be okay with each season that I am in has made me stronger. To be an anomaly and to allow my true purpose to flow through me has required me to think differently. I have to be open to new possibilities, to allow my mind to see and flow in new ways, and to welcome things that I didn't know yet. Going outside of the borders, and being willing, even in a state of sheer desperation, to try something new, can immediately give us new life and open our eyes to things we've never even imagined.

There is a time under heaven, chosen by heaven, for a purpose. That means that as it is in heaven, is God's desire and will for us here on earth. He never created a day that He wants us to lack in. He hasn't created any seasons of opportunities that He desired for us to fail in. But our human journey created a new dimension, and He is designing those as well to work for our good.

God brings all things together beautifully for His glory, and many times, for our enjoyment and capacity to be enlarged. Being okay with who we are and learning to grow our uniqueness to its greatest potential will not only affect each of us personally, but it will empower all of us collectively.

One who deviates from that which is accepted is not one who is in rebellion, but rather, one who is in creation. Think about that for a minute. Learning to create within your anomaly state opens up doors that very few have walked through, because ego and judgment haven't allowed it. But we're in a new era where we are now going beyond rights to identity. Beyond war to unity. Beyond feminine or masculine. As a woman and a successful businessperson, one of the most significant things I have learned is that the feminine and masculine were never meant to operate without each other. They are conducive to each other and bring out the best of each other as we operate in both. This is not to say that we all change who we are to operate more fully in the feminine and the masculine, but it means that we are open to being our fullest self, remembering we were created in God's image, who is both masculine and feminine, and at the same time, is neither. Being an anomaly in all of this uniqueness will heal all of us if we're willing to open our own hearts first.

Grab a Journal!

What are your dreams? Let your pen start pouring out all the dreams that you may have dismissed because of age, income, gender, your strengths or weaknesses, or other reasons that you've always believed were holding you back. Now take some time and visualize these. Shut your eyes and allow your mind to take you there. Pay attention to every detail. The more you do this, you'll even start to pick up smells, sounds, and more. Focus on your strengths and what could get you there! Write it all out.

ANOMALY ACTION: RELEASE YOUR GIFTS

It took an anomaly to create the very first phone, which took our communication to new places. It took another to create the first portable phone. Then we went cordless. Before we knew it, we were able to speak to each other while we were away from home! Then we had a computer in our pocket and a music library we could access anywhere in the world. Anomalies are always breaking boxes, expanding thoughts, and changing the dynamics of the things we do. In other words, anomalies are unstoppable when they share their God-given gifts. How about you? Are you ready to release your gifts? I deeply believe that God has designed each of us uniquely and has given us gifts to share with the world.

Yet, one of the most devastating things that can occur when you have a gift is to feel alone. To feel that you are different and that it is somehow a bad thing. You don't fit in. You feel like you don't belong. To me, that feeling of being different, of not having a sense of belonging, is a call from God. He is asking us to live at a higher level. To be not what others expect, but rather what He has created us to be.

I can tell you that many times I've prayed while lying on the floor of my office and sobbing my eyes out to Papa and begging Him to make me free. I think without knowing it at the time I was asking Him to let me see myself as He created me. To be free to be myself.

I want to share what I've learned in those moments when I felt broken and alone so you don't have to feel that way.

1. Never live your life alone. You were not created to be on your own. Even if you have negative people around you who don't believe in your dreams, you can connect with supportive people through the power of a smartphone and an Internet connection. God didn't create you to be alone. Reach out, and please, find compassionate people to connect with. Trust me, there are good people out there who can and will relate to who you are. Seek them out.

2. Never give up on your dreams. God, whether you believe in Him or not, didn't create you to live a meager existence of going from one act of survival to the next. God designed you to dream and live a life that is beyond yourself. There are people who desperately need your dreams to ignite. Write your dreams down, visualize them, focus on your gifts, and continue to move forward in what God has given you. This is your destiny.

3. Seek out remarkable people who are living their dreams and who share your gifts. Whether it's a mentor in marketing or copywriting, in music or in science, strive to work with someone who has the unique strengths and abilities to help you realize your dreams. Find someone you can connect with spiritually, emotionally, and professionally. Seek a mentor who speaks truth, speaks to your potential, and will love you through every single phase of your journey. This is why I created my Inner Circle academy—so I could not only provide tangible business support, but also help people who are pushing against boundaries to live outside the box! And through that loving support I wanted to make sure they wouldn't lose who they are in the process.

4. Live in faith and prepare for a joyful and successful life. Don't doubt your purpose and the One who put you here to live it. Look at me. When I thought my life was over and the last saga of my drama was about to unfold, God blew a new plan and a new life right into me. He reached down and took a woman who had experienced both shattering pain and enormous success, and He gave her the desire to go even further. I am here to tell you that right when you think the wild and ridiculous can't happen, you'd better start packing your bags for the journey!

RESISTANCE: THE ANOMALY MIND-SET

As you begin to embrace your anomaly mind-set, you will get closer to living your true purpose. At first, this will feel empowering. I say "at first" because at some point, you will start to have doubts. Resistance is painfully reliable. But by now, you will recognize resistance when it shows up right on time as you're beginning to truly celebrate who you are. Just as you start to accept and love yourself as the beautiful and amazing anomaly that you are, you may feel the need to pull back. To hide your light. To conform.

Don't. Instead, lean on faith. That's what I have done and will continue to do.

Faith will take you further than anything in life. Faith in the impossible, faith that will believe against all odds. Faith in the future despite what the past said and the present is saying. Faith will get you past resistance and into the person you were always meant to be.

My friends, please hear me when I say this: you are worthy of being loved. And love is stronger than resistance, and it always will be. You are perfect and you are beautiful, and while we've never met, I love you. We are connected, you and I. Papa God created us both and brought us together through this book.

He created us as anomalies. We are different. We don't fit the mold. We don't conform. But that is not because we aren't supposed to be here. That is the lie that we tell ourselves, the lie that society tells us. But it's false. We are meant to be here! As catalysts. Game changers. Disruptors. To stir things up. To move the world forward. We are necessary. We are needed. We are exactly who we were created to be.

But in order to access the incredible power God has given us through our uniqueness, we must accept that we have been given gifts. We are here to share our gifts. The world needs us to see ourselves as God sees us, not as society does.

So, adopt an anomaly mind-set. If society perceives something about you as a deficit, you must view it as an asset. Think about that. Do you know how unstoppable you can be when you shift your mind-set this way? Take that, resistance!

> ### Spiritual Takeaway
>
> I am created with a purpose, and the tension I feel is proof that a border needs to be broken or reinvented. My mind is a beautiful and powerful thing, and I am worthy of being loved.

CHAPTER 10

LIMITLESS

God told me I was limitless many years ago. He also said "invincible," but I didn't believe Him. I wonder how many times heaven has spoken a word over you to empower you, or even identify your gift and calling, but you ignored it. Me too. I did that for many years, while building huge businesses. This is an important point I must make—you can have all kinds of success and still never hit the potential that you're called to. Just because you can do more, go further, and get more done than the rest of the people in your life, that doesn't mean you've tapped into your limitless power yet.

The difference between walking in the limitlessness of heaven and all I've been given vs. doing things on my own and trying to make things happen, is energy. It also was the difference between renewal and strength and utter exhaustion for me. I can play the role I'm assigned. With the trauma I've endured in my lifetime it wasn't hard to become a professional actress in the screenplay of my own life. But learning to walk in my truest nature, revealing my real self to the world, and allowing heaven to flow through me was a whole new dimension.

To be limitless is to be without end, boundary, or limit. There are no constraints, no borders, no boxes, and energy that never ends. So many of us deplete our energy trying to fit in, conform, and be someone we're not so others won't feel threatened or be jealous or critical of us. The trouble is, this drains most, if not all, of our limitlessness. The artificial boundaries and boxes must be broken, and it's important that we pay close attention to the self-talk we give ourselves day in and day out. We are creating every day, with our thoughts and our words, the things we believe.

I recently had a stem cell transplant. It was in my knees, as I've had bone-on-bone issues for 14 years. Also in my neck there are four disks that keep slipping and creating problems, but seven doctors refused to operate because of my medical history. Then the stem cells were injected into both of my shoulders, as I've been working with a 60 percent tear, spurs, and arthritis for over 10 years. Lastly, an IV infusion systemically helped my colon and entire body. Here's the clincher: they took stem cells from my own adipose fat and then placed them back into my own body. SELAH. That means "think on this" in the Bible. Think on this. The cells I needed to grow new cartilage, heal my gut, restore my strength, eliminate spurs, and regenerate me were already in my body.

Here's a truth I pray you get. Please, stop what you are doing right now and read this very slowly. I *already* am whole, complete, and lacking nothing. I *already* have everything I need. My hair is standing on end as I write this. The presence of Papa God in my living room where I'm writing in the early, early, dark hours of the morning is very thick and tangible. I'm praying it transfers through the pages of this book, or the audio you're listening to, and touches you too, right where you are at. I *already* have everything. YOU already have everything. YOU are already whole, complete, and lack nothing. You were born that way, to be a creator.

The war begins at a very, very young age. Someone speaks to us about something we did, how we look, sound, or act, and our broken identity starts. If it is not in agreement with all that heaven has spoken, we become fractured. We hear that we are lacking and we believe it. We are told that we are not enough and we live like it. We feel and receive judgment and we identify with it. The fractures begin. The trauma lodges itself into our DNA. Then *everything* we already have to live a vibrant, successful, powerful life is being attacked by everything we don't need. Everything we don't want. Have you felt like you are in a war? Well, I'm here to say you are.

HEALING

I went through some healing with the Restoring the Foundations Ministry, which I mentioned earlier, and we discovered that I had multiple fractured parts. This doesn't mean I have multiple personalities. It does mean that the whole, unbroken, complete, and lacking-nothing state that God created me to thrive in had been fractured to the point that my wounds were crying out from my muscles, memories, and more. Triggers happened almost daily. This is where hypervigilance set in. I'm happy to share with you that we healed all those parts, and the dramatic transformation that people can see I went through on social media has much to do with that healing. When the triggers stopped, and the healing continued, it's incredible the things I began to see in the spirit realm, feel in my heart, and all that I was able to create with my restored mind!

Our brain records the comments, insinuations, facial expressions, sounds, and more that people give us. We keep track of the messages in the media, of paintings on the wall as we walk by, from the atmospheres where we work, and everything else we encounter all day long. This great "recording" that our brain does begins to reinforce the lies. But the human brain was *designed* to reinforce the truth and to make us a powerful creator. Unfortunately, because of pain, trauma, and mixed messages, we're recording things we were never meant to experience.

When we repair the fractured parts, and come face to face with all that we've been given, the love of God becomes so evident. He is for us, and not against us. He gave us everything—in life, through Jesus, for our past, present, and future. We are no longer orphans, groping through life, crying out for someone to love us back to health. We are now sons and daughters, walking in our inheritance, living in our power and experiencing life at a whole new dimension. This, the fact that we're *not* living as everyone else does, creates friction. Remember that if you ever feel unliked. That feeling does not come from being different. The truth is, you are so powerful that you leave an impact everywhere you go.

There is nothing that can come close to the love of God. His love satisfies at a level that no one, or nothing else, could even dream of being. It is in this space when we see who we are, when we see whose we are, and we see all that is surrounding us in the realm of heaven, that we can go farther, recover faster, and be more than we ever dreamed was possible.

Cory Asbury has an album titled *Reckless Love* that I've been listening to while writing this book. There's one song on there, "Your Love Is Strong," that I urge you to listen to. It means something so personal to me. The song speaks to how our insecurities can be overcome by love. God's love. It is the greatest force on our planet. Love does win. It will always win! The love of God is so strong that it picked me up in my weakness and remade me. It's so strong that it broke the cage that trauma had me in, and opened my voice again so that I could write this book. To many people hearing all the things I went through, they'll feel encouragement, but then look at their own lives and say, "That's amazing for you, but it's impossible for me."

But it is possible, because this is who we are. This is the truest essence of who we are, who we were meant to be, and all that creation spoke into existence when God had His first thought of us.

ALWAYS LIMITLESS

We are many things—each of us. God made me an apostle, one who leads, and sends out. I'm also a business owner and a mom. An excellent wife (waiting for a husband presently) and a brilliant daughter. I'm a friend, a teacher, and someone who knows how to laugh at the struggles and see in the future something greater. At this season in my life I don't have any limits, or so it seems. I truly feel limitless. I feel no entanglements or financial issues. But the truth is we are limitless even when we feel limited. When we feel the most entangled, disrupted, ungrounded, and lost, we are still limitless. Isn't it fascinating that I could be in so much pain, but tucked away deep inside of my DNA and stem cells was everything I needed to be healed? It just needed to be activated.

We can no longer be just an information-consuming society. We can't be the "I am trying to find my identity society." We need to become the society that *did it*. We made it happen, we got it done, we went farther, even when we felt like crap! Even when we feel at our most broken, fractured, unable, and incapable— even then we are limitless. We need to pursue healing, no matter what it takes, because it's the right we were born with.

CALLED

I feel called to lead a limitless movement. I feel like I'm ready to give birth. I can't carry this message alone, this is not something that I can even manifest alone. We are one and must do this together. Our limitlessness is waiting! It's taken me so many years of my personal journey to truly understand what Papa meant when He said, "You are limitless. You are invincible! You are an ANOMALY." Now it's my honor to help all of you. The only reason I have shared my pain and some deep issues of my story is to give you hope. If I could live through that and be here—the question becomes, what can you do? Now that you know you are unique, wired for a purpose, and are supposed to never fit in, where does this leave you?

How shall we live if we can do anything?

Take a few minutes with me right now. Be still. Really still. Still enough to hear yourself breathing. Keep on breathing slowly. In and out. Relax your muscles. Quiet your thinking brain. Go to your heart. Right there. Some of you are crying now. You try so hard every single day to not go there. This is where your sorrow has lived for a long time. This is where desire died many years ago.

God recently reminded me that to create we must start with *desire*. This is why Resistance, the devil, and all the forces of darkness go after our desire in a full-on assault. Could this be why we crave and desire things that can destroy us? We're created for intimacy, but we crave something fake. We are designed for community, but we hide away. We are made to be limitless, and even our DNA proves it, but we repeat the messages of our past over and over again. How shall we live, then, if we can do anything, but we're struggling to even do something?

God looks for people who will trust him. The Bible says He searches throughout the earth every day looking for someone who He can show Himself strong on their behalf! My best advice for you is this: Raise your hand! But what if you suffered through horrific trauma, pain, and abandonment over and over again, just like I did? Maybe you lost several babies to miscarriage, just as I did. Or you're dying inside because no one knows you're suffering in an unhappy marriage, just like I was.

Or maybe you are sick of taking painkillers. You're not addicted, or maybe you are. I wasn't psychologically addicted, but my body was physiologically dependent. So while I might not have had the strong mental struggles, urges, and cravings that an addict has, my muscles, brain, and the chemicals in my body had to relearn how to live without opiates. No one came and waved my pain away. I wasn't willing to live in pain every single day. So I took matters into my own hands, and began to do everything possible to help my body heal. Maybe you're there right now but you have no idea where to start.

The first step is raise your hand! I asked Papa over and over again for the solution. He led me to relocate, try new things like medical cannabis, test out dry desert heat, explore things like acupuncture, remove trauma from the body, and more. But *none* of this would have happened if I had not believed these two critical things:

First. That I am limitless and I deserve this. These are fighting words for the religious. They'll tell you that you're dying, perishing, fading daily. "You are not limitless and you need to just trust God and give it your best." Then they'll remind you of what you really deserve—hell and suffering. They'll paint a horrific picture of a hateful God and remind you that you deserve *nothing*, so just take what you have. That, my friend, must leave. That must break. I invite you to say that now! "I break these lies off of my mind, body, and soul right now in Jesus's name!" *You* were created to be limitless. Even the very cells in your body prove it to be so. Sure, you might age. Yes, you are going to die. But while you are here on this planet called Earth living your life, you have everything you need. You deserve all that Papa God gave you. He's the one who put the limitless stem cells into your body. He's the one who created you to *regenerate, restore, and renew*. Get into agreement!

Secondly, believe. We hear this all the time, but it's true. Neuroplasticity means that nothing will ever change if we don't believe that it can change. Belief is a key component to neuroplasticity working. Expecting good, believing for the best, and giving it our all work together to synergistically create for us the life we deserve and were made for. God so loved the world that He gave His son Jesus for us. He also gave all things that would ever pertain to our life. Look it up. It's in the Bible. BELIEVE.

Now I realize that there's no other book in the entire world that has caused more pain for people than the Bible. Yes, I did just say that. In every church across the globe, you'll hear that it's the most powerful, life-changing, life-giving book around. But maybe, like me, you've had so many scriptures and verses quoted at you that even the word *scripture* triggers you. It did me for me too, for a long time. The verses that were used to hurt me, humiliate me, and to put me in a category of no repair were many. This book has been misused, abused, and used to bring harm, where God intended healing. It's caused people to believe lies that are straight from the darkness. This is why I say that no other book has caused so much harm, when misused by men and women. But it was written with this intention—God LOVED the world. He didn't send Jesus or anything to condemn us, rather to save us. Meditate on this: the most powerful book that can set us free became a book where resistance destroyed lives, homes, and careers that God wanted to thrive. Isn't it time we take back all that we lost?

DREAM WITH GOD

God is looking for people who will co-create with Him. We are designed to create! It's time for us to become the people we were meant to be. Heaven never asks for us to be perfect. No, that's a lie and distortion from men and women. God asks us for faith—perfect faith that won't doubt or listen to the lies.

Learn to dream with God.

Let Him take you to places in your heart and mind that you have yet to even see or experience. One of my favorite ways of doing this is to get really quiet in the early, early hours of the day, and put on some great music and just lie on the floor. I call this "soaking." I don't ask for anything, am not requesting anything—no conversation, just *receiving*. I let the songs wash over me like the waves do when they crash onto the shoreline from the ocean. The words crash over me, fill my mind with truth, and give my mind something to "record" that is more powerful than all of the lies I've heard, seen, and experienced.

Many times when overwhelm or weariness tries to set into my workday, I'll do the same thing. Find a quiet place, put on the music, lie down, and let it crash over me. I'm meditating on the words, receiving them into every cell of my body. Papa God does the rest.

When I would be plagued with fear and doubt, and the flashbacks of trauma I've lived through race through my mind at will, I would then dream with Papa about a day free of pain. A day free of suffering. NOW. Not later. This was not a day that would come as so many had said after I died. How morbid is that thought? Struggle like hell here on earth and then when you finally barely make it to heaven, God will wipe your tears and tell you "well done." Who the heck created this psychopathic view of God? He said that sometimes we'll have to give up things in this life, for us to be the best that He created us for. Then we're promised that if we have to give up anything, He'll give us more, IN THIS LIFE, and beyond. It doesn't say He'll just repay us, bless us, and encourage us in heaven. (Matthew 10:29.)

What kind of Daddy would He be if he only rewarded us once our lives are over? That's morbid. It's not appealing. Yet over and over again people fall for this lie and nonsense and miss out on the greatest truth ever—Papa is in a good mood and is on your side NOW. Here in this life now, every single day with you, He is for you and not against you. He really is! Jesus rose from the dead. He said it is FINISHED. It's time we start acting like it is, and reject these lies of all that we need to be before God will love and accept us.

Here's the truth: I am a miracle.

Truly. There's no way I should be able to do what I do every day at work, without Papa doing a miracle. My mind and heart were broken into a million pieces. No one could put me back together. Not medication, not meditation, not anything. But when the great love of God came in, He did a big work that would never be forgotten. It's kind of funny how people tell me all the time, "You are so easy to remember!" As I began to dream with Papa and build a new life, a lightness, a brightness, and a limitlessness that I'd never know before was birthed. It is this that I think people remember—the energy, the freedom, the anomaly. I declare that God wishes to do a big work in your life as well.

Allow yourself to dream again.

Have no desire? Then ask God to restore it, heal your lost desire, and make you into something brand-new. I dare you to pray that right now. Train your mind to go to places you've never been to before, to see yourself in the future without any restrictions, and in the present well, able, and growing. Let your child brain come to life again. Receive the pictures, numbers, sounds, scents, and other things that heaven wants to send to your senses. This is not just for children. We were made to be creators and co-creators with heaven!

When the questioning, reasoning, and assessing come in, just take a deep breath and get into agreement with heaven. There will be times for questions. There are plenty of times you'll need to compare pros and cons and reason your way through things. But in order for you to learn how to do that with all of heaven's help, it's important now for you to BELIEVE that you can.

Faith will take you farther than hustle will. While I believe in hard work, discipline, and commitment, I subscribe to the belief that positivity will take you further than negativity. I know we must be self-disciplined and self-governed to get anywhere in life. Because I've dealt with chronic pain and illness for most of my life since childhood, I get it that we have bandwidths, commitments, and relationships. But faith will still take us further. Faith is a complete trust and confidence in something outside of and beyond ourselves. When I sit in a chair I have faith that the thing will hold me! While this might not be the same kind of faith that causes me to heal my pain, it is still at its very core, faith.

CREATE JOYFULLY

Count it all as joy, my friends, when you experience difficulties and struggles. Throw a party! Get balloons! I know that sounds insane, but the truth is, at the end of every difficulty is more wisdom, knowledge, and, if we allow it to be, grace. If we didn't have any struggles, we'd never know how strong we are.

When I came back to the gym after not working out regularly for more than 20 years, my entire body thought I was insane. The muscles screamed so loud I had to use topical pain cream as a body lotion many days. It was hard to walk the length of my subdivision, which is very small. Doing my own bodyweight for squats almost killed me. The fire was hot, the pain was screaming, and the swelling was horrific. I couldn't wear half of my jeans or shirts after a good workout because of the swelling. But I don't swell like that anymore. Now I get a PUMP into my muscles and within a few hours it goes down. As my body begins to heal and recover, it is getting stronger. I can now do 10 reps with the Smith Machine upside leg pressing 360 lbs.! HELLO!? I can now do over 150 lbs. on the hack squat and over 380 on the leg press. I'm a CREATOR. I'm creating the kind of life, body, and future I want. So can you! That's what we were given. I BELIEVE that my body knows how to restore and heal itself, and it's shown me it does. The struggle it took to go from massive soreness, feeling super out of shape and like I didn't belong in that gym, to now knowing I'm in great shape, got my body fat down below 18 percent (at 55 years old!) and that I met some of my best friends at the gym is the process of moving from struggle to strength.

BIG-PICTURE LESSON

For some of you, going from heartbreak to loving again will be the greatest battle you'll ever fight. But you deserve to be loved even if you've never really experienced it before. For others, living without chronic physical pain is your destiny and to get there you'll need patience, hope, courage, faith, and a thorough understanding of neuroplasticity. To get to the future you want, while eliminating your past, and staying present in the now, will be the greatest battle you will ever fight. But please, fight it. We need you to step into your limitlessness. Remember this in your war—we're programmed to disassociate. We've been trained to hold back. Millions of people around us every single day are basically sleepwalking. But that doesn't mean that we have to be like that. *Faith* will take us further.

What is your limitless goal? What is your heart and mind calling out to you? I want you to take some time and journal all that you're thinking, feeling, and processing right now. Don't let it evaporate into the atmosphere. Be very specific. Nothing becomes tangible and alive until it becomes *specific*. This is where we dream, fly, and soar. This is what we were made for! This is how we were wired, created, and designed. But life has taught us otherwise. Experience has made us cautious and guarded. Words have been spoken over us that must be eliminated. Lies must be uprooted and removed. So get really specific. Let your mind and heart see the pictures. Breathe in the scents. Your brain is a marvelous creator and longs for you to go to levels you've never gone before.

We're designed to be creators, with God and with others. This is one of the biggest reasons that our purpose and calling goes far beyond just "us." Its impact in the lives of others can't even be seen right now. Never in a million years did I know that this is where I'd be today. When I was building my first business, believing God, pressing past my pain, and working super hard to create a new life for my family, writing this book and having this wisdom and knowledge was not even a speck of a thought in my mind. But I knew in my heart of hearts that I was created for more. I felt the yearnings; a constant fire was burning inside of me and crying to be set free! The limitlessness cries out. It longs to be set free. You've felt it, I know you have. When you're working, playing with your children, fighting your way through this week's struggles. There's something more that cries out! Maybe you've heard in church that you should just be content. Maybe others have tried to pacify you with their own disbelief and told you to not be so hard on yourself. It could be that you have even taken inventory of all you've done, all you have, and decided that enough is enough. Survival set in.

My friend, you were not meant for survival. You're an overcomer and you're an anomaly who was made to create and grow.

ANOMALY ACTION: TEN GUIDEPOSTS

Being limitless means more than you are beyond being limited. It means you are now creating new expansions in the things you do. This mind-set requires that you are open to change. And change takes courage. Here are the ten core lessons of this book that I pray you will have the courage to adopt in your life and your business:

1. Conquer your obstacles. Regardless of how unlikely your success may be in this moment, decide you will achieve incredible results. Make a decision ahead of time about what results you will achieve. Write it down. See it. Post notes around your home and office. Record it in your mind. The word *decision* is very unique and very strategic. It comes from Latin, meaning, "to cut off." So decide today to detach yourself from the limiting beliefs that restrain you. You may need to cut off toxic friends and family members or put bigger boundaries on them! Do whatever it takes. You are worth it.

2. Partner with God for supernatural success in business and in life. I could not have gotten to where I am now without partnering with Papa God. He has no limits on how many business partners he will have, so get in agreement with Him and expect results. Wait, make the miracles! Miracles can happen in your life every single day. Ask for them. Believe for them! You'll be amazed by the changes that belief can create.

3. Accept your past and ask God to help you forgive those who have belittled and hurt you. They did not understand you. Resentment is a poison that brings you suffering, not the one who harmed you. Ask God to help you feel compassion for the hurt people who have sought an outlet for their pain in you. People who are hurt cause hurt and pain for others. Refuse to receive that pain again. Instead move away from whatever pain lives in your past. Forward is your new direction. You don't need anyone to understand you, approve of you, or accept you to be whole. You are already whole, entire, and lacking nothing. Forgive. Move forward. Remember that your strength will inspire and equip someone else!

4. Deviate from the norm. When presented with a challenge, embrace your anomaly mind-set and see the possibilities instead of the problem. Give yourself permission to do your thing because your thing might be birthing a movement. Tell yourself there is a solution, even though you may not see it right away. Seek solutions more than problems. Pray on it. God will open your mind to the possibilities for creation in your challenge. Always remember, you are a creator, not a survivor who is simply struggling along.

5. Refuse to be limited by any religion that constrains your relationship with a loving God. If your religion is a source of joy and love, that's wonderful! But if it is a place in which you feel condemned, be very wary. Let no one come between you and God. Find a new church. Find new friends. Seek the truth and you will find it! Ask God to reveal Himself to you. Ask Holy Spirit to show you the way. I believe you will experience things beyond anything you've ever imagined. My prayer is that you would ENCOUNTER God, not just know of Him. His love is strong.

He's the friend who can calm the storms in our souls. He is close enough to remove all the insecurity. When fear is crippling, He'll be the safe place, and a place we can run to when our world feels like it's crumbling around us. In your darkest hour, He'll raise you up again. I believe that for you!

6. **Shine.** When you look back on your life until this moment, no doubt there will be many memories in which you felt isolated and different. In the past that may have been a source of great pain. Make a shift right now. Realize that you are not a misfit; you are a miracle. Say it out loud. "I am a miracle." God sees that. It's time you did, my friend. Your uniqueness is a gift to all of us. It's critical you lay aside any desire to fit in and renew that with a desire to *shine.*

7. **Claim your birthright.** We've all heard the dream-crushing question, "Who do you think you are?" Now you know the answer. "I am a unicorn. An anomaly. A miracle." That's right! You have been designed by God to share your gifts with the world. That's who you are. You're not like anyone else. The love of God made you so different that when you walk in your truth, all your enemies will be eliminated, and the freedom that is your birthright will shine forth.

8. **Bring love with you every day**, into your life and your business, whether it's a job or you're an entrepreneur. Love your co-workers, love your challenges, and love those customers of yours who make it possible for you to do work that you love. Love will change everything about your life and the work you do, if you just let it. There is nothing more powerful than love. Love always wins.

9. **Define your own success.** Don't be fooled into thinking that achieving a business goal or making a certain amount of money is the definition of success. It is not. I am NOT a success because I am wealthy. I am a success *because I am free.* Free to be truly, unapologetically myself. Free to use the gifts God has given

me every day. Free to spend time with people I love who nurture my soul. That is what I wish for you. Freedom.

10. Know that you are limitless with God. When you accept yourself for who you really are, you are unstoppable. God has put no limits on you. So, please, my friend, take off the limits you have placed on yourself. They are not real. They do not serve you, and they do not serve the world. Define your potential as limitless. Know that all things are possible with God and that everything others have labeled as weird or quirky about you— well, those are your divine gifts, my friends. Use those gifts with faith. Unlimited faith.

RESISTANCE: STAND WITH GOD

When you set out to achieve the dreams Papa God has made possible for you, resistance will show up like never before. Its job is to crush your dreams, to stifle your spirit, and to ensure you stay stuck. Knowing that gives you power. Remember, resistance is the lie that says, "Just settle." Resistance says stay silent even when the fire inside of you is crying out to speak. It's a murderer. It's a destroyer. But you are LIMITLESS, and you no longer listen to the voice of resistance. Oh, you can still hear its taunts in the background, but your focus is elsewhere. Seize that power and carry it with you on your journey to supernatural success. Expect obstacles. Expect setbacks. Expect your dreams to feel impossible. But resistance will never win. Because you won't be facing it alone anymore. Now you will be standing with God, in your authority as someone who not only dreams of a future that would have been impossible for you before—you see that future. You feel that future. You own that future.

Resistance doesn't stand a chance. Faith is carrying you now.

Spiritual Takeaway

You are limitless in what you can dream and what you can achieve by embracing your uniqueness, and understanding that everything is possible with God. Onward, my friend. You are unstoppable.

CONCLUSION

My Prayer for You

My dear readers, I could have never gotten to where I am if it were not for all of heaven surrounding me when I felt so alone and so unable to do all that the dreams in my head had told me to do. But God—He brought me through. He carried me, empowered me, and gave me courage to breathe again every time I felt so out of breath in this race called life.

So now, I want to bless you and remind you that you can do all that God designed you to do. You are powerful, you are strong, and you are well able.

God, I pray you would open the eyes that are shut through pain and fear, and let them see again all of the dreams you designed for them to fulfill. Open their ears to hear things from heaven that we need for them to bring to earth. Awaken the dreamers, I say, come awake and breathe again! May the visions not be aborted; may the strategies not be thwarted. God, I pray you will surround them with angels and give them a hope that doesn't burn out through all that life will throw at them.

I impart to you the grace, courage, and wisdom that God gave to me, in wisdom and in life. Freely it was given. I didn't deserve it. I never, ever earned it. And in many ways, I was never trained for it. So I pray that all of heaven would impart to you now more wisdom than I have, more grace, and more courage. God told me to ask Him for the nation of Facebook, that we might all become one, bringing forth this war of life and love. I pray that you too will have supernatural favor in your ads, on your videos, in the content you create, and most importantly, that you'll connect with people that need you. May you go farther than you could ever go on your own.

I bless you from the top of your head to the bottom of your feet. I bless your family, your children, your grandchildren, and all that concerns you. May your business prosper in ways that don't make sense and may your story be just like mine, a "you cannot make this stuff up" kind of story that empowers and encourages others.

In Jesus's name. Amen!

ACKNOWLEDGMENTS

This book would never have been possible without the encouragement, support, and "cheering me on" of some very important people.

My first editor, Mary O'Donohue . . . how do I ever thank you enough for all you've done for me? You saw the unicorn way before I did, the vision God gave you aligned with all He had shown me; and most importantly, you gave me the courage to not let go when I wanted to quit, multiple times. I love you and am so honored that you carried this journey with me. Thank you for helping me keep my ten books into one topic, for fanning my flame, and for bringing together all the words that were written backward, in spirals, and incomplete.

To my sons, Jeremiah, Justin, and Bobby: You gave me a reason for living. A reason for going on when I saw no hope or reason within myself. We grew up together; we lived, loved, cried, and created together. Now, you're grown men with lives of your own, and as I look back on everything I've done in life, all the goals accomplished and the dreams fulfilled, seeing you rise up in freedom to your destiny gives me more joy than anything else life has to offer. I'm so proud of you and will forever thank God for making me your momma. You are my why, my reason for living, and the reason I always hoped and saw a better tomorrow.

Jeremiah, you were God's gift to me as a single mommy, and when I had so much shame, you came with your bright light to remind me of heaven's great love and fullness. Your beautiful mind has challenged me and given me faith to become all that I am. Through all of the years of building businesses together, I'm so grateful for all the words, the faith, and the prayers you spoke over me to simply be who God made me to be. You gave me a love for fast cars, dreams that go beyond the galaxy, and the courage to chase my dreams because I deserve to do so! I love you more than I could ever find the words to say.

To Justin, my middle son, who carries peace and wisdom. The justice that God poured into your heart has reminded me so many times to keep the first things first. I love that you know how to keep things in order and you know when to turn the music up super loud and dance it out! You're a protector, a warrior, and the fires God caused for you to put out and bring back generations of people who forgot who they are is yet to be seen, but written in the book of the story of your life. Cigars and a sip of cognac are special times I'll always remember with you. I love you more than words can say.

To Bobby, my caboose, my chill pill, the one who reminds me to dance and that everything really will be okay. You've inspired me to dream bigger than ever before and you reminded me that little boys grow up to want to marry someone just like their momma. This has motivated me to be the best version of myself in life and in business, and, more importantly, to have wonderful quality time with people I love. You're my diva son who loves to shop with me, and showed me how to color outside the lines. But most importantly, you're the one who gave me the courage to dance wildly before God no matter what life throws at me! I love you more than words could ever express.

To Abigail, the woman who helped me to come out of my outdated fashion closet, who saw a beauty before I did, and forever spoke life over me, even when I was still learning. You came in as an assistant and made order out of my chaos and joy out of my frustration, and you always knew when to bring me a Starbucks and a muffin so I could get done what had to be done, no matter how I felt that day. I will forever be grateful for how you served me, supported me, and loved me. Thank you for teaching me how to love myself as a powerful, beautiful woman. I couldn't have picked a better wife for my Jeremiah—you're a gift to us all.

To Holly, the bright light who has always been shining, believing in me, cheering me on, and reminding me that God will carry me through. The visions, dreams, and words that God gave you will be memories I'll never forget. The mirror with Jesus looking back at you, giving us hope for the future and that everything will be okay. Your pure heart has inspired me to be a better woman. You're a gift to Justin, and I'll never forget the first time we met and I knew you'd be his wife.

To Q: You came into my life when I least expected it and gave me the courage to be the anomaly God made me to be. Your friendship and love have opened closed parts of my heart, and have given me faith to share this story around the world. Thank you for all the dinners where we talked and dreamed about all we could do with this message, for being one of the best friends I've ever had and for supporting and encouraging me as I turned the music up real loud and let my creativity grow again. You are a gift I will cherish forever.

To Momma Danice and Papa Gary, the parents that God sent to love my heart back to health. You saw the big dream of this book long before I even wrote the first word. You've believed in me, prayed with me, cried with me, danced with me, celebrated with me, and reminded me to PARTY MORE! You are the embodiment of the mothering and fathering heart of God to me, and I am forever changed because you loved me with an unconditional love.

To Sister Mary Katherine, my third grade Catholic teacher, who told a very broken, hurting little girl that I could fly higher than I ever imagined if I would just believe. I'm flying! Look at me now!

To my literary agent, Sharon Bowers, for helping me weave through my million book ideas, for believing in me when I wanted to quit, and for all the early-morning and late-night texts that helped me to walk by faith, and not my feelings. You're more than an agent, you're a sister, and I am so grateful we are aligned together.

To my family at Hay House, you opened a hidden door that God had for me and have given me a place to shine bright. I will forever be grateful and honored to be a part of your family. Special thanks to Editorial Director Patty Gift for believing in this message and making a place for me. Thanks to Mary Norris who helped me bring my heart and words together on the pages so that people could find out who they are. Thanks to Editor Sally Mason-Swaab for helping all this come together to become this great work that is much bigger than me. I value you and the opportunity to work with you.

Almost last, but definitely not least, to the millions of people who follow me on social media and who are more than just followers—you are family. Some of you have become team members in my companies, others have become some of my very best friends in the world. You helped me to show that there's no difference between a virtual and a real world, and we've grown so much together through the last 10 years. You inspire me, give me hope for a better future, and have reminded me that together we are so much more powerful than we could ever be alone. You're the anomalies that changed my life and gave me courage to write this book, and to share some of my own story.

Finally, to my very best friend, my DNA, the One who knows me, loves me, believes in me, has never ever left me alone, and created me in my mother's womb to break all rules, be unique, and shine a light that at times it seemed the world was not even prepared for . . . Papa God, you taught me how to love. You gave me hope to live again and believe again. When you told me to ask you for the sword of Joan of Arc, I never dreamed that it would come through in this book. You told me to remind people who they are, and to tell them that what you have said in their heart, they can do. I love you with a love that is forever, and I'm so glad I now know *I am your girl.*

ABOUT
SANDI
KRAKOWSKI

Sandi Krakowski is an "outside-of-*every*-box" author and speaker, top social media influencer, thought leader, and culture creator. Her specialty is embracing faith at work, empowering women, and creating culture and marketing for brands.

Krakowski, a woman who started her first multimillion-dollar company as a young mom, has overcome many of her own obstacles, personally and professionally. She is the founder and president of her current multimillion-dollar empire: A Real Change International, Inc. and Sandpaper Tablet, Inc. Krakowski takes pride in the fact that these companies conduct business in ways that bring faith into the workplace, bringing together happiness, kindness, faith, and strategic principles that bring results for business owners and employees.

Krakowski has spent more than two decades working successfully in online marketing and business development. A noted Facebook marketing expert, she was named in *Forbes*'s "Top 20 Online Marketing Influencers of 2014," "Top 20 Women Social Media Influencers," and "Top 50 Social Media Power Influencers" lists. She also writes for *Entrepreneur Magazine*, and has been featured in *Forbes*, Mashable, American Express OPEN, and Beliefnet. She has helped build 15 notable companies by utilizing her experience in eCommerce, Internet marketing, direct-response marketing, publishing, book creation, copywriting, sales and management, team development, and leadership.

In addition to empowering and equipping her online audience, Krakowski enjoys spending time reading books, working out, hiking, traveling, drinking good wine, and eating chocolate. But her favorite thing is to spend time with her sons, Jeremiah, Justin, and Bobby; her daughter-in-loves Holly and Abigail; and her absolutely edible grandson, Luka.

CONNECT WITH SANDI

Instant Access to This Exclusive Members Only Social Media & Marketing Video Vault You Can Use Anytime, Day or Night to Make More Money Fast!

You Get Access to:

- Copywriting secrets to increase conversion
- Social media marketing strategies
- How to brand yourself online
- Facebook ad writing secrets
- Money-making marketing steps for beginners
- How to set up your social profiles
- E-mail marketing tips
- Writing better headlines and tags
- **Over $7,497 in training content that was previously only available by consulting with Sandi privately**
- _150 unique videos_ on every topic of doing business online
- Facebook ads templates
- Social media engagement map
- E-mail marketing swipe file

Absolutely FREE!
No Strings, No Obligation, No Credit Card Needed!

https://www.arealchange.com/money-vault/

The Inner Circle Mastermind & Small Business Academy is the place where success happens! Includes everything you'll need to attract the right customers, grow a profitable and sustainable business, and live the life of your dreams!

Over $70,000 in Complimentary Training & Classes!

- NEW! Access to over 67+ full-length classes that Sandi has done!
- NEW! Over 5 years of Inner Circle Archives in The Vault!
- Weekly video training and assessment of businesses from Sandi Krakowski personally
- Get your questions answered with Q & A Day!
- Action Steps you can take in your business each week
- Live interaction with Sandi in her Private Facebook Group for Inner Circle Members
- Weekly LIVE Webinars with Sandi as a group with fresh content EVERY single week!

The Inner Circle Mastermind currently serves over 2000 active students and is where you can get one-on-one access to Sandi every week for your business needs.

www.arealchange.com/innercircle

TALK WITH SANDI

Sandi's social media community serves over 1.5 million people just like you! You can connect with Sandi and speak to her personally on her social channels:

Facebook:
www.FB.com/sandikrakowskibiz

Instagram:
www.instagram.com/sandikrakowski

Twitter:
www.twitter.com/sandikrakowski

Sandi's Offices in Phoenix:

Mailing Address: 3145 E. Chandler Blvd.
Suite 110-350, Phoenix, AZ 85048

Office: (888) 938-4703 Fax: 574-822-4813
Hours: M-Fri 9AM – 5:00PM CST

Hay House Titles of Related Interest

THE SHIFT, the movie,
starring Dr. Wayne W. Dyer
(available as a 1-DVD program, an expanded 2-DVD set, and an online
streaming video)
Learn more at www.hayhouse.com/the-shift-movie

***

*CLAIM YOUR POWER. A 10-Day Journey to Dissolve the Hidden Trauma
That's Kept You Stuck and Finally Thrive in Your Life's Unique Purpose,*
by Mastin Kipp

*DO LESS: A Revolutionary Approach to Time and Energy Management for
Busy Moms,* by Kate Northrup

GET OVER IT!: Thought Therapy for Healing the Hard Stuff,
by Iyanla Vanzant

*HIGH PERFORMANCE HABITS: How Extraordinary People Become That
Way,* by Brendon Burchard

*WOMEN ROCKING BUSINESS: The Ultimate Step-by-Step Guidebook to
Create a Thriving Life Doing Work You Love,* by Sage Lavine

All of the above are available at your local bookstore,
or may be ordered by contacting Hay House (see next page).

***

We hope you enjoyed this Hay House book. If you'd like to receive our online catalog featuring additional information on Hay House books and products, or if you'd like to find out more about the Hay Foundation, please contact:

Hay House, Inc., P.O. Box 5100, Carlsbad, CA 92018-5100
(760) 431-7695 or (800) 654-5126
(760) 431-6948 (fax) or (800) 650-5115 (fax)
www.hayhouse.com® • www.hayfoundation.org

———

Published in Australia by:
Hay House Australia Pty. Ltd., 18/36 Ralph St., Alexandria NSW 2015
Phone: 612-9669-4299 • *Fax:* 612-9669-4144 • www.hayhouse.com.au

Published in the United Kingdom by:
Hay House UK, Ltd., Astley House, 33 Notting Hill Gate, London W11 3JQ
Phone: 44-20-3675-2450 • *Fax:* 44-20-3675-2451 • www.hayhouse.co.uk

Published in India by: Hay House Publishers India,
Muskaan Complex, Plot No. 3, B-2, Vasant Kunj, New Delhi 110 070
Phone: 91-11-4176-1620 • *Fax:* 91-11-4176-1630 • www.hayhouse.co.in

———

Access New Knowledge.
Anytime. Anywhere.

Learn and evolve at your own pace
with the world's leading experts.

www.hayhouseU.com